CAMBRIDGE
through student eyes

Written and produced entirely by students
The essential guide to the historic city of Cambridge
Insiders' guide to wining, dining, entertainment and nightlife
Walks and places to visit in and around the city

EDWARD II

Editor: Maddy McTernan
Publisher: Emma Horton
Typeset in-house in Bembo and Caslon 540
by Tim Harris

Published by Varsity Publications Ltd
11-12 Trumpington Street, Cambridge,
CB2 1QA

The contents of this publication are believed to
be correct at the time of printing. Nevertheless,
neither the Editor nor the publishers can accept
responsibility for errors or omissions, or for
changes in details given.

The Publisher has been unable to trace the
copyright owners of certain photographs repro-
duced in this book. Any persons with such
information are requested to contact The
Publisher, Varsity Publications Limited, 11-12
Trumpington Street, Cambridge CB2 1QA.

ISBN 0 902240 21 8

First published 1991
Second edition 1993
Third edition 1997

Produced by: Ennisfield, Telfords Yard, 6-8
The Highway, London E1 9BQ

CAMBRIDGE
through student eyes

CAMBRIDGE
through student eyes

University
City

Historical Cambridge

B efore there was Gown, there was Town. There has been a settlement of sorts on the banks of the river Cam since Roman
times. The bridge, from which the town takes its name, was
built by the Saxons in the 7th century.

After the Romans left, the river (known to the Saxons as the
Granta, and today as the Cam) divided the kingdom of the Mercians
from that of the East Angles. The Saxons called the town
Grantanbrycge, the Normans called it Grantebrigge, Chaucer called it
Cantebrigge.

The Backs

The river itself was the main source of the town's wealth; winding
through the fens (the swampy marsh land to the north of the town), it
eventually joined the Ouse. Barges bringing goods from all over north-
western Europe stopped at Stourbridge (where a huge annual fair was
held from July to September), Midsummer Common, and the Backs
(the fields behind the colleges which run down to the river). Visitors
gliding along the Backs in chauffeured punts are following the course
taken by barges well into the 19th century; in the 18th century, one
Master of Trinity College used to bring the produce of his rectory to
his private granary on the river behind the College.

There is a long history of competition between the universities of
Oxford and Cambridge, although when it comes to arguments over
which is the older it must sadly be admitted that Oxford probably has
the advantage, the more fanciful inventions of generations of
Cambridge scholars notwithstanding.

It is well documented that in 1209, following the killing of an
Oxford student by some townsmen, the scholars went on strike. This
was a serious business; in mediaeval times, the presence of a band of
scholars in a town meant lucrative trade. The resulting diaspora of
Oxford academics settled in several towns, but only in Cambridge did
the settlement become permanent.

This immediately led to trouble. The scholars did not just bring
their learning with them but also a hostile attitude to the townsfolk.
Though the University was as yet unofficial, it assumed all the traditional rights of such a body. Conflicts grew increasingly fractious – one
Chancellor even excommunicated the Mayor – and the University's
hand was strengthened when in 1318, at the urging of Edward II, it was
officially recognised by Pope John XXII.

Relations with townsfolk reached their lowest ebb in 1381, when a
mob led by the Mayor and burgesses sacked most of the University

buildings, and burnt all the documents they could lay their hands on with a cry of "away with the skill of the clerks!" Retribution for these acts was swift, and came in the form of the King granting the University control over many aspects of the life of the town, including the pricing of bread, wine and ale, the checking of weights and measures, and the licensing of entertainments, rights which the University retained until the 19th century.

Most of the colleges, those communities which distinguish Oxford and Cambridge from most other universities, were founded in three waves. The first wave, founded from 1284 to 1352, were simply student halls of residence; St Peter's (or Peterhouse) was the first, followed by Michael House and King's Hall (both of which became parts of Trinity College), Clare Hall, Pembroke Hall, Gonville Hall, Trinity Hall and Bene't Hall (now Corpus Christi College). Several of these still survive, though only Peterhouse and Trinity Hall retain their original names; the rest have become known as colleges, or have been refounded under different designations.

The second wave occurred in the Tudor age, from 1441 (when King's College was founded) to 1594 (Sidney Sussex). Ironically, many of these colleges (Queens', Trinity, St John's, Magdalene and Jesus) were built of red brick. The third wave has occurred over the last hundred years or so, and, reflecting the extensive changes which occurred in the University in the 19th century, includes the foundation of colleges for women and research students.

St John's College
Old Bridge

Like all mediaeval universities, Cambridge was home to scholars in all four of the great faculties of theology, medicine, law and the arts. Students wandered from university to university in search of the greatest teachers of the day; Cambridge was home to students from all over Europe. The Dutch scholar Erasmus, perhaps the greatest scholar of the Renaissance, taught at Queens' College between 1510 and 1513. He didn't enjoy it much, complaining incessantly about the cost of living in Cambridge (plus ça change), but he did like the women of the town, whom he called "divinely pretty, soft, pleasant, gentle, and charming as the Muses".

The conflicts that engulfed England over the next two hundred years were mirrored in Cambridge. During the 16th century, Cambridge became a hotbed of Protestantism, many of her alumni being burnt at the stake for their faith in the 1530s and 1540s. Clashes between Papists and Protestants were a regular feature of University life through much of the century. One hundred years later, Cambridge was again rent in two, by the Civil War this time; the division being along the by now traditional lines of Town (who supported Cromwell) and Gown (who supported the King, despite claiming Cromwell as one of its alumni). Not surprisingly, the University suffered under the

Protectorate, but regained its position when Charles II was restored to the throne. This was also a period of great advancement of learning; to name but one participant in this process, Isaac Newton, discoverer of gravity, lived and worked at Trinity College.

The 18th century is commonly regarded as the nadir of the University's history, a period when students and scholars alike did little other than drink, gamble and carouse. It is certainly true that the energies of the University were not directed towards teaching, but this was because, at no other time in the University's history, have its affairs been so intimately bound up with intrigue, influence, and all the other aspects of the new party politics. By the end of the century, however, the long neglect of its academic basis had begun to affect its reputation. Samuel Taylor Coleridge, who came up to Jesus College in 1791, wrote, "In Cambridge there are sixteen Colleges that look like workhouses, and fourteen churches that look like little houses. The town is very fertile in alleys, and mud, and cats, and dogs, besides men, women, ravens, clergy, proctors, tutors, owls, and other two-legged cattle."

**The Cavendish
Laboratory site**

A traveller from 1600 would have found much of the University of 1800 very familiar. The University's primary function was to educate the minds of young men who would enter the church; the study of mathematics was considered to be the best way of achieving this. By 1900, however, everything had changed. The town expanded and, with the coming of the railway in 1845, became more cosmopolitan. The University underwent an enormous expansion, both in numbers of students and the range of subjects taught. Students no longer had to be members of the Church of England. Extra-mural examinations were instituted. Lecture courses and examinations were opened to women. The traditional faculties were supplemented by laboratories of science, both pure and applied, teachers of multifarious languages both living and dead, and diverse new philosophies. All this change came under the influence of outside competition (the University of London was founded in the 1830s), outside scrutiny (Royal Commissions in the 1850s and 1870s), and a reforming instinct from within, which one historian has called 'the revolution of the dons'.

The changes set underway in the second half of the 19th century gathered pace at the beginning of this century. Burgeoning numbers of research students found a home in the University. The reputation of the University's scientific departments – particularly the Cavendish Laboratory and the Institute of Biochemistry – grew and grew, numerous Nobel Prizes being garnered by scientists educated or based in Cambridge. Women were finally admitted to degrees in 1947 and, in the 1970s, the colleges began to go mixed (the last all-male bastion being breached when Magdalene went mixed in 1988). Students campaigned for a voice in the academic affairs of the University; an effective University-wide Students' Union developed in the early 1970s.

It is easy to see Cambridge as a place of unchanging tradition and beauty, but this is far from the case. Today, in the 1990s, the pace of change is as rapid as ever. New departments are being created, and old ones renovated, funded by a massive development appeal, to keep Cambridge at the forefront of the academic world. The academic centre of gravity of the University, which has shifted over the centuries from the Old Schools, and is currently split between the Science area next to Downing Street and the Arts site on Sidgwick Avenue, is set to shift yet again to West Cambridge, where green field sites are earmarked for University use.

The University Today

C ambridge has no campus, but rather a collection of colleges and academic departments. All students are junior members of one of the 31 colleges (six colleges are devoted to graduates, and three are for women only). Many, but not all, of the University's academics are also fellows (senior members) of one of the colleges. The college is the centre of the undergraduate's life: it provides accommodation, food, individual tuition, pastoral care and entertainments (usually organised by the students themselves).

The departments are responsible for organising lectures and (where appropriate) practical work for undergraduates. Each department has its own library. Most departments run seminar series and academic meetings to which a broad range of researchers contribute — from nervous PhD students giving their first ever paper, to leading figures in each field. The departments are grouped together into faculties; these bodies co-ordinate the teaching curriculum, set examinations, and judge the quality of research submitted for advanced degrees.

The power of actually granting degrees rests with the University, rather than the colleges or departments. Degrees are given at a ceremony held several times a year at the Senate House, on King's Parade. The largest of these ceremonies is the General Admission to BA degrees, spread over two days at the end of June, at which nearly all the final year undergraduates (some 3,000 in all) receive their degrees; by a curious quirk of Cambridge tradition, all undergraduates receive BA (Bachelor of Arts) degrees, even if they have studied a scientific subject.

Behind the Senate House are the Old Schools. These buildings housed the faculties and the University Library until the early 19th century; they now contain the University's administrative centre. The University Library moved from this site in 1934 to its modern home across the river, the work of Giles Gilbert Scott. The Library is one of the country's five copyright libraries, entitled by law to a copy of any book published in this country. Whilst in practice the Library does not

The University Library

actually take every book, it does have an enormous collection of over 4 million volumes (many of which are very rare, or even unique), as well as extensive manuscript holdings.

A significant proportion of the books held in the University Library were published in Cambridge by the University Press. The Press dates back to 1534, when it was granted a charter by Henry VIII. The Press was once housed in the Pitt building on Trumpington St, built in 1833 with the surplus from public subscriptions for a statue of William Pitt (Prime Minister 1783-1805). Although it still maintains offices in the building, the Press has now moved most of its operations to new premises near the railway station. The church-like appearance of the Pitt building's façade led to its being dubbed 'the Freshers' church', after the hoax played on generations of Cambridge freshmen who were informed that their presence was required there on the first Sunday of the academic year. Even today, one may spot the occasional bemused, gowned student outside the building on the second Sunday in October.

The University is a self-governing body. The position of Chancellor is, and has been for many centuries, largely ceremonial. Real influence rests with the Vice-Chancellor, who presides over the Council of Senate, which is made up of senior fellows of the University. The Council's proposals – known as 'graces' – are debated by the University's resident fellows. A vote is held upon a matter if, when the grace is read out, one of the fellows says "non placet" ('it does not please'). The reports of the Council of Senate and the graces are printed in the *Cambridge University Reporter*, the official university journal; although the *Reporter* is not supposed to carry any controversial material, it does have an 'unofficial' section in which the often heated debates are closely reported. The Vice-Chancellorship used to be a part-time job, held for two years by one of the Heads of the Colleges; due to recent changes in the University's administrative structure, the present incumbent, Professor Alec Broers, is the second full-time Vice-Chancellor.

Professor Alec Broers

Discipline is maintained within colleges by the Dean, who has the power to fine offenders if he sees fit. At a University level, the officials responsible for discipline are called 'proctors'. The job of proctor is today far less onerous, and far less dangerous, than in the past. In years gone by, the proctors would patrol the city's streets, wearing gown and mortar board, accompanied by two 'bulldogs' (burly porters who could catch, and restrain, unruly students), checking that students weren't frequenting undesirable hostelries, or committing the truly heinous crime of not wearing their gown.

(left) St John's Bridge of Sighs

The Colleges

Much of the charm of central Cambridge stems from the intimate character of the college courts and the beauty of the ancient buildings. The most picturesque of the colleges are the oldest, mostly to be found along the river and around the city centre. These are all within a short walk of each other, mostly along the Backs. Each college has its own distinctive character and unique history, explaining the way it is today.

Colleges are generally headed by a Master or a Mistress, except for King's (a Provost), Queens', New Hall, Wolfson and Clare Hall (Presidents), Newnham (a Principal) and Robinson (a Warden). Other senior members of colleges are usually called Fellows. All are elected largely on the basis of their academic achievements. Most have heavy teaching and administrative duties, but all regard their research as equally important.

The number of students in each college varies from fewer than 100 to nearly 1000, of which usually two thirds are undergraduates. Most colleges house all their undergraduates, and students may find themselves living in rooms that are centuries old.

Visitors should bear in mind that the colleges are places where people live and work. For this reason, parts of many of the colleges remain closed altogether in the examination period in May and June. In addition, groups of ten or more people wishing to tour the colleges must be accompanied by a blue-badged Cambridge guide. Details are available from the Tourist Information Centre.

The Ancient Colleges

Peterhouse

Peterhouse was founded in 1284 by Hugh de Balsam, Bishop of Ely, predating all other colleges by over 100 years. Unfortunately, the only remaining building from this time is the Hall where breath-taking examples of William Morris' stained glass and tiling can be found, although these date back only to its 1831 restoration. From the front, the college appears much less imposing than many of its neighbours because of the slightly mixed up layout. However, although home to only 200 students, the college's land stretches along the rear of Trumpington Street. Of the many students who have enjoyed their time here, the most famous include the poet Thomas Gray and the scientists Henry Cavendish and Charles Babbage.

Pembroke – Lying just across the street from Peterhouse, Pembroke can claim the first building to be completed by Sir Christopher Wren; the college chapel. Founded in 1347 the college has a particularly relaxed feel to it. The Courts are open and seem more like gardens than the starkly manicured lawns that many colleges favour. This probably partly explains the popularity of its summer garden parties, for which students can often be seen queuing down Trumpington Street.

Found outside the library is a statue of William Pitt the Younger who became Prime Minister aged 25, only ten years after he began his studies at Pembroke.

Corpus Christi – Continuing towards the centre of town from Pembroke the next college you will come across is Corpus. Corpus Christi is unique as the only one of the Cambridge colleges to be founded by townsfolk. Old Court provides an excellent example of mediaeval architecture and dates back to when the college was founded in 1352. Most of the rest of the college was not built until 1823, by the prolific architect William Watkins whose services Corpus shared with Downing and King's. Christopher Marlowe is the college's most famous student, and in fact it was here that he wrote *Tamburlaine.*

Old Court, Corpus Christi College

St Catharine's – Affectionately known as Catz by its students, is located just opposite Corpus. The college was founded by King's provost in 1473 on land just to the South of its more famous neighbour. Most of the college dates from rebuilding completed in 1775. The front gate looks onto Trumpington Street and looking into the college from there the three closed sides of a typical, if uninspiring, courtyard can be seen. Previous students have included Dr John Addenbrooke (founder of the city's hospital) and William Wotton who entered the college in 1675 aged nine and already fluent in Latin, Greek and Hebrew.

Queens' – named in honour of its two founders, it is located on Silver Street. Originally founded as St Bernard's college in 1446 by Queen Mary of Anjou (wife of Henry VII), the college was renamed and further work carried out on it by the wife of Henry VII's successor, Queen Elizabeth Woodville. Cloister Court is a beautiful Elizabethan courtyard dominated by the half timbered President's lodge. The College is divided by the Cam, the two halves linked by the mathematical Bridge. Many tour guides will tell you that this was built under the direction of Newton and originally did not need to be held together by nuts and bolts. This, however, is not true; Newton died 22 years before the bridge's construction.

King's – Situated in the middle of King's Parade this magnificent structure provides one of the most famous sights in Cambridge. William Wilkin's ornate gatehouse and King's Chapel stretch halfway along King's Parade overshadowing their neighbours; the neo-classical Senate House and St Catharine's. It was Henry VI's aim to build a huge college with an arcaded front court, bell tower and a cloistered court on the backs. Although the college was founded in 1441, and work started on the Chapel five years later, Henry VI's overthrow meant that most of the site remained empty for more than 300 years. This dismayed the locals who remembered the buildings that stood on the site before they were razed to make space for the college. It did take considerably less time to complete the Chapel, even though this task still took 69 years.

The Chapel draws huge numbers of visitors each year, including a film crew from the BBC each Christmas to film King's College Choir carol service, broadcast annually on Christmas morning. Sightseers are also attracted by Rubens' Adoration of the Magi, anonymously donated in 1972 which hangs behind the altar. Sadly, the most impressive and famous building in Cambridge is now in need of restoration where acid rain has begun to cause damage. In 1996, the college launched an appeal to try to raise the millions needed to carry out the work.

As well as its magnificent architecture, King's also attracts a lot of attention for the student protests staged there over the last couple of years, mainly concerning student poverty. Consequently, King's students have the reputation of being the most politically active in Cambridge.

Clare College

Clare was founded in 1326 and looks onto the back of King's. This college didn't enjoy the most successful start, as lack of funds forced it to be re-founded by Lady Elizabeth de Clare only 12 years later. Few of the original buildings remain due to a fire in the sixteenth century, so the buildings you can see now originate from the 17th century. Clare can boast the oldest bridge in Cambridge, decorated with stone balls. An old trick is to ask how many balls there are. The correct answer is 13 and four fifths as one has had a segment shaved off.

The Fellows' Gardens are some of the prettiest open to the public and can provide somewhere peaceful to relax if the bustle of the town is becoming too tiring.

(left) King's College

Trinity Hall – After the devastation caused by the plague, Bishop Bateman of Norwich founded Trinity Hall to train a new body of lawyers and priests. That was back in 1350 and since then Tit Hall (as it is colloquially known) has produced many eminent judges and lawyers. To this day it is still respected for its legal training. Unfortunately, Tit Hall is another college to have suffered fire damage and most of the 14th century main court had to be rebuilt or re-surfaced in 1852.

The novelist Henry James described the area around the Elizabethan library as the prettiest corner of the world. It is also worth taking a quick look inside the library where Jacobean bookcases contain the original texts that have been chained there for centuries to prevent theft.

Tit Hall's Chapel may be the smallest in Cambridge but was completed in 1352 and now contains stained glass commemorating Robert Runcie, the college Dean between 1956 and 60, who later became the Archbishop of Canterbury.

Gargoyle, Gonville and Caius College

Gonville and Caius – Found at the end of King's Parade, this college is known as Caius after its founder, John Keys, who latinised his name, thus causing confusion to tourists and first year students alike before they realise the correct pronunciation is simply 'keys'.

Cauis originally dates back to 1348 when it was founded as Gonville Hall by Edmund Gonville. After Henry VIII snatched much of the college's land for his new college, Trinity, Dr Keys refounded it as Gonville and Caius in 1557. Dr Keys provided many of the delightful features the college is now known for, including the three gates to symbolise his ideal of a student's career. The Gate of Humility is now to be found in the Fellows' Garden; the Gate of Virtue provides the entrance to Caius Court; and the Gate of Honour (decorated with sundials and crests) leads to the Senate House. Caius students still walk through the gate of Honour to the Senate House for their graduation ceremonies.

Trinity – There are many things that Trinity is famous for: its size, its wealth, its alumni – all of which have given birth to many legendary stories.

It began with Trinity's famous founder, Henry VIII, who in 1547 ordered the amalgamation of two existing colleges (King's Hall and Michael House) to form the largest Cambridge College. Thomas Nevile worked on much of the college and created the Great Court,

(right) Trinity College, across the Backs

consisting of over two acres of lawn surrounding the fountain that once provided the whole college's water supply. Among the Tudor buildings is the clock tower, immortalised in the film *Chariots of Fire* where a race was held around the outside of the court while the clock struck twelve. Eton was the actual location used in the film, but the race is re-created each year after a college feast – first year students attempt the Great Court Run, unexceptionally without success.

Behind the Great Court can be found Nevile's Court, which Nevile left open to the river that runs just behind it but which was closed off in 1695 by Sir Christopher Wren's library, now one of the city's most famous buildings. The library houses many original manuscripts, including works by Milton, Wittgenstein and AA Milne, amongst the limewood bookcases. From the outside it is not possible to judge the library's size due to Wren's effort to conceal the height of floor level. Standing under the library it is also possible to re-create Isaac Newton's experiment when he calculated the speed of sound. Just stamp your foot and listen for the thunder-clap echo.

Trinity is the biggest Oxbridge college, as well as the richest. Rumoured to be the third biggest land owner in the country, a popular myth is that you can walk all the way to Oxford on Trinity's land. More trustworthy facts about the college include that it has produced six British Prime Ministers and more Nobel Prize winners than the whole of France.

Crest, St John's College

St John's – Positioned right next to Trinity, there always has, and always will be, rivalry between the two. This is most apparent during the Bumps rowing races in the Lent and Easter terms. St John's Boat Club was renamed Lady Margaret (after Lady Margaret Beaufort, the college's posthumous founder) at the turn of the century. It is rumoured that this followed an unfortunate incident when Trinity's cox was killed as their boat was bumped by John's, who had fixed a sharp spike to their stern. Now, every morning before the races, crews and supporters of each boat club congregate in their respective college for the 'stomp'. The two groups march through their own college before meeting on the Backs, where there is much jostling as each club attempts to capture the opposition's cox. Usually not much more than a college scarf is captured which is then hung from the top of the college boat house.

The College was founded in 1511 and consists of a series of distinctively different courts. The First and Second Courts, in Tudor style, adjoin the 17th century Third Court. The gothic 19th century

(right) The Pepys Library, Magdalene College

New Court (known as the Wedding Cake) is linked to the older parts of the College by Henry Hutchinson's Bridge of Sighs, an exquisite imitation of its namesake in Venice. The newest building is found behind New Court; this the Cripps building completed in 1967. Despite looking somewhat out of place in its ancient setting, the building (which provides accommodation for students) won awards for the innovation of its design.

Magdalene – Another example of confusing pronunciation that will catch out anyone who is not familiar with the city: Magdalene is pronounced 'maudlin'. Situated next to Magdalene Bridge, the college is most famous for housing Samuel Pepys' 3000 volume library. Formerly a Magdalene student, he left the collection to the college on his death in 1703. Still there, in its original red oak bookcases, the most highly prized treasure is Pepys' personal diary. Written in a secret code, it took three years to decipher. The college was founded in 1428 as Buckingham college and originally only housed monks. It had to be refounded in 1542 by Lord Audley of Walden after the college suffered losses as a result of Henry VIII's programme of dissolving monasteries.

The Magdalene of today still has a reputation as a very traditional college; at its annual May Ball female guests are required to wear dresses that will not reveal their shoulders or their ankles. Magdalene was the last college to admit women, holding out until 1988, and only caving in as the college's academic results slipped compared to the results of other colleges who admitted both sexes.

**Jesus College;
'The Chimney'**

Jesus' spacious grounds once belonged to the Priory of St Radegund in the early 12th century, before the Priory fell into disrepute and was refounded by a college. This was in 1496, thanks to John Alcock, the Bishop of Ely. The gatehouse stands at the end of a walled passage (nicknamed The Chimney), and through this First Court is found with the bronzed horse statue in the centre.

The Chapel, restored in the 19th century, contains ceiling designs by William Morris and some pre-Raphael stained glass. The college has several celebrated alumni including Prince Edward, Thomas Cranmer and the journalist Alastair Cook. Less celebrated at the time was the poet Samuel Taylor Coleridge, who was eventually sent down for bad behaviour and bad debts.

1996 was Jesus' Quincentenary and the college marked the year with one of the biggest and most ambitious May Balls ever; over 2,000 guests dined in huge marquees in the college grounds.

Sidney Sussex – A fairly small college located in the city centre, most well known to students because it is opposite the supermarket, earning it the nickname 'Sidney Sainsbury's'. The Countess of Sussex, Lady Frances Sidney bequeathed £5,000 to found the college on the site of a friary in 1596. The 16th and 17th century buildings were given their current appearance by Sir Jeffrey Wyattville in the early 19th century when he created the two uniform courts that front the college.

Despite its mundane nickname, this college probably boasts the most interesting legend of them all. Although Oliver Cromwell was a student as Sidney, the college supported the King in the English Civil War. After the Restoration, Charles II ordered Cromwell's body be exhumed and beheaded, but it was not until 1960 that it was re-buried. The head was given to the college and now rests in an unmarked location in Sidney's Chapel, buried amidst great secrecy with the Master, the Chaplain and three Fellows looking on.

Christ's – Now located at the bottom of St Andrew's Street, Christ's was originally intended to be God's House situated where King's now lies. Displaced by Henry VI's plans to build his huge college, Christ's moved to its current site in 1446 but was not renamed and refounded until 1505 by Lady Margaret Beaufort (also the founder of St John's). The majority of students live in Sir Denys Lasdun's New Court built in 1966, who have nicknamed it 'The Typewriter'. Poet John Milton studied at Christ's, known as 'the lady of Christ's' by his fellow undergraduates. Charles Darwin, author of *The Origin of the Species* is another of Christ's many famous alumni. Within the University, Christ's has a deserved reputation for academic excellence, due to its position at the top of the University league table that compares the examination results of each college. Non Christ's students are often heard enviously attributing the success to the strict rules that forbid televisions in students' rooms and insist on the closure of the college bar at 8.30 each evening.

Emmanuel – A little way along St Andrew's Street is the 18th century entrance to Emmanuel (affectionately known as Emma). Another college founded on the site of an unfortunate Priory dissolved by Henry VIII, Sir Walter Mildmay (Queen Elizabeth I's Chancellor) created it in 1584 as 'a seed-plot of learned men'. He hoped it would provide priests for the newly established Protestant Church. The original Priory buildings were adapted to reflect the changes in religious thinking; the old church was converted into a dining hall and the refectory into the Chapel. But the new Chapel was never

Front Court, Emmanuel College

consecrated, and was replaced in 1677 by the current Chapel in First Court, designed by Sir Christopher Wren. Sir Walter's original aim was a success; many of the first Protestant settlers in New England were graduates of the college, including John Harvard, founder of Harvard University.

Sidney Sussex was the last of the ancient colleges to be founded. It was not until 200 years later that any more colleges were established, the first of these being Downing in 1800.

The Younger Colleges

D owning College can be found on Regent Street, five minutes up from Emma. Due to legal wrangling between the family of its founder, Baronet Sir George Downing, and the University, the building of the college was greatly delayed (and the legacy greatly reduced). Work started under William Wilkins in his neo-classical style in the early 19th century, but the college remained unfinished until modern times. Downing's style differs from the other colleges; Wilkins moved away from the traditional courtyards to a lawned campus style which pre-dates that favoured by some American universities. Downing is recognised within the University for its rowing prowess, its Women's 1st Boat is often Head of the River, therefore hosting the ceremonial boat burning.

Downing was one of the last colleges to be established for general educational purposes according to the ancient tradition. Subsequently, most colleges have been founded to perform a particular educational need in Girton's case to provide University education for women.

G irton, two and a half miles from the city, was the first of the women's colleges. Originally located in the Hertfordshire town of Hitchin, it then moved to Girton Village, felt to be a safe distance from the man of Cambridge. In 1978 the college admitted its first male undergraduates.

N ewnham was the second college for women, established in 1871 after Henry Sidgwick, a Trinity Fellow, rented houses to provide lodgings for female students. The college received its Charter in 1919, although it was not until 1948 that women were recognised as full members of the University. Newnham does not have its own Chapel, being strictly

Newnham College

(left) Downing College

non-denominational but the college does have the University's first building to have been designed by a woman. Elizabeth Whitworth Scott's Fawcett Building was named after Philippa Fawcett, who gained the highest marks in the University's maths examinations in 1890 despite not being awarded a degree because of her gender.

S elwyn – situated next door to New Hall, was founded in 1882 to make provision for those who intend to serve as missionaries abroad and to educate the sons of clergymen. Students were originally required to have been baptised as Christians, and fees were kept very low through public subscriptions to encourage poorer students.

H omerton College is Cambridge's teacher training college, relocated from Homerton Village in Middlesex to the outskirts of Cambridge in 1894. Homerton stopped admitting men in 1897 and only agreed to re-admit them as recently as 1978.

Homerton College

The Modern Colleges

N ew Hall was founded due to the success of a society that was formed with the sole aim of establishing a third Cambridge college for women. They succeeded in 1954, with the college originally starting out as a limited company situated near the Backs. New Hall later moved to its present site in 1964. The most striking feature of the buildings (designed by Chamberlain, Powell and Bon) is the huge white dome over the dining hall, famous within the University ever since undergraduate pranksters painted big black footprints over it.

F itzwilliam (found next door to New Hall) existed for almost 100 years as Fitzwilliam Hall for students who were not members of any college. It actually received its Charter to become a University college in 1966 when it moved to its current location from its former site at the other end of the town. Famous ex-Fitz students include British politician and ex-Master of Emmanuel college, Lord St John of Fawsley, and the Singaporean leader Lee Kuan Yew.

C hurchill is the national monument that honours Sir Winston Churchill. It houses a selection of his papers in its Archive Centre, including a number of his personal writings,

Churchill College

(left) New Hall

controversially bought and donated to the college with money from the National Lottery. The college opened in 1966 as an all male college but became the first male college to admit women six years later. The college was established to address the problem of Britain's shortage of scientists, therefore a large proportion of its students are studying science courses.

Robinson is the newest college. A gift of £18 million from its single benefactor, Sir David Robinson ensured its establishment as the only Cambridge college founded with students of both sexes in mind. The college was opened by the Queen in 1981 and occupies a twelve acre site near the University Library.

Cambridge University also comprises six other colleges. Most of the were founded over the last two centuries for graduate students or mature undergraduates. Hughes Hall, Darwin, St Edmund's (most famous for being the college where many of Cambridge Blues rowers study), Wolfson and Clare Hall are all mainly for graduate students. Lucy Cavendish is unique in Europe as the only college specifically for mature women who wish to resume their studies in any discipline.

University
Life

A Year In Cambridge

Michaelmas term

October – The Cambridge academic year commences at the beginning of October – later than at most other universities – and each of the three terms last only 8 weeks, considerably shorter than everywhere else (except Oxford). This would lead some to believe that Cambridge students have it easy and do less work than other students. but this is not the case. The University's unofficial motto is 'work hard, play hard' and you have to with all your work, sport and socialising crammed into such a short time.

Term starts with Freshers'Week.This is the week when all the new students arrive and are introduced to Cambridge life before lectures begin. Each college's student union will organise its own activities for the first years, usually including drinks parties, meals and pub crawls. Many colleges also assign each fresher a college 'family' consisting of two second or third year students who can show their 'children' around.

The Societies Fair

One place all freshers go during this week is to the local sports hall where the Societies Fair is held. Inside the bustling hall members of every University society stand at stalls recruiting members for the new year, offering incentives ranging from the ever popular free drinks to flying lessons. There are hundreds of societies to choose between, from the cultural and the charitable to sports and silliness.

Further into term Matriculation Dinner is held by all the colleges. This is a formal college feast where new students are ceremoniously welcomed into their college by its fellows.The meal often consists of at least four courses and everyone is expected to wear academic dress (gowns).This is often followed by much less formal drinks parties held by Tutors for their new students.

November – With lectures and supervisions well under way, November offers the chance to settle down and train for all the sports you were persuaded to take up during Freshers'Week. Nearly everyone at Cambridge tries rowing for the college at some stage – most often in the first term. Rowing is taken very seriously with many colleges having 5 or more men's boats (with 8 rowers and a cox in each boat) and at least 3 women's boats, all of whom train at least 4 times per week.This term is viewed as a training term to coach all the new rowers and spot talent for the higher boats. This culminates in Fairburns, a race at the end of term which novice boats can enter.

(left) Cambridge times

Also during this time, many intercollegiate sports tournaments, Cuppers, begin. This often means two matches each weekend for hockey, football or rugby players.

December – The Michaelmas term ends early in December and this is marked by many colleges by a Christmas dinner, as well as the traditional pantomime staged by Cambridge's two foremost dramatic societies, the ADC and Footlights. Adapted from traditional stories the pantomimes are always sold out, always very funny and never suitable for young children! The pantomime has been held at the ADC theatre for decades, where many of Britain's most famous comedians (for example, Emma Thompson, Stephen Fry and John Cleese) started their careers.

Another Cambridge institution is King's College Chapel Choir who are filmed each year by the BBC, singing carols in the famous Chapel, to be broadcast on Christmas morning.

The beginning of December is also interview time, so as the current students leave, hopeful candidates arrive to compete for places (dependent on school exam results) at Cambridge the following year.

The last big Cambridge event before Christmas is the annual Varsity rugby match held against Oxford. The match, played at Twickenham, is televised around the world and the cameras often show crowds of student supporters with faces painted in traditional university colours, Cambridge's light blue and Oxford's dark blue. Many of the players seen here go on to compete internationally – it was only a few years ago that the Cambridge side contained Gavin Hastings and Rob Andrews, who went on to captain England and Scotland respectively.

Lent term

January – Cambridge looks very pretty in the snow, but when the students return from the Christmas break it is bitterly cold, as the wind blows in from Siberia. Now is the time when many decide that getting up at six am to get to the boat house at first light is torture, and the boat clubs lose quite a few members.

Queens' College students during the rag procession, which heralds the beginning of 'Rag Week'.

In January elections are held, both within colleges to choose the new members of the college student unions, and to elect the officers of the University Student Union. At college level, the agendas of some candidates are often based more on the opening hours of the college bar and the drinks it serves than on the more serious issues dealt with by the University Union.

The fund-raising work of Cambridge Rag starts now. In order to raise money for charity, students get involved in Rag organised fun events such as Rag Blind Date and Rag Assassins. The latter involves being assigned a target (another student), with the aim of shooting them with a water pistol. A prize eventually goes to the assassin who 'kills' the most of his or her fellow students.

February – The Rag activities culminate this month with the annual hitch to Europe. All the fancy-dressed hitchers meet up in a European city and have to raise as much money as possible on their way there.

In the fourth week of this term, the second college feasts of the year are held. Halfway Dinner is not as formal as either Matriculation dinner or Graduation Dinner, but is held as a celebration for second years halfway through their courses who cannot go to either of the other feasts that year.

March – The highlight of the term for those rowers who lasted through the winter is the Lent Bumps. This one of the two major collegiate rowing races of the year (the other being the May Bumps). All college boats have places in one of eight divisions, and for four days all seventeen boats will line up a length and a half apart according to their positions in the division. They race to catch up with the boat ahead – all start as the starting gun is fired. This often leads to confusion and sometimes accidents and chaos as boats attempt to hit each other. A bump is scored if you catch the boat ahead of you before the boat chasing you hits you. If this is completed successfully, the boat moves up a place for the following day. In the higher divisions, where all the crews are very fast, there is often not much bumping, however, in the lower divisions results can be spectacular as the differences between crews can be great, resulting in boats actually overtaking the boat they were chasing and bumping the boat ahead of them. This is an over-bump and the crew moves up two places.

Boat-burning at Trinity Hall

In the evening of the last day of races each college will celebrate its success with a Boat Club Dinner. Special celebrations will be held in those colleges of the Clubs that are top of the Men's first and Women's first divisions at the end of the competition. These colleges celebrate being Head of the River by burning a wooden boat in the grounds. It is also traditional for the triumphant crew to jump over the boat as it blazes.

A safer activity has to be going to see the Marlowe Society's annual production. The play is usually professionally directed and is often a heavyweight production. (Marlowe's *Tamburlaine* and Ibsen's *Peer Gynt* that recently been featured.)

April – Rowing remains the focus well into the Easter vacation as the build up to the Boat Race starts. Although college rowers are now spectators rather than participants, the event is a very important one in students' diaries as they congregate (often in pubs) along the course of the race between Putney and Mortlake on the Thames.

The boat race is always a hotly contested national event that Cambridge crews have won convincingly in the last few years. A particular triumph was in 1993, when Cambridge beat a semi-professional Oxford crew captained by Olympic gold medallist, Matthew Pinsent.

Easter term

May – A very quiet month due to the exams held at the end. Most people work hard and hectic social lives are temporarily put on hold as studies become tense. (It is also worth noting that many colleges close their doors to visitors during this period.) However, the end of exams is celebrated in spectacular fashion.

June – The first Sunday after all the exams are over is a day for garden parties and relaxation. Societies at different colleges hold parties in the Fellows' Gardens serving fruit punch and fresh strawberries to their guests, who relax in the sun and listen to the jazz bands organised by their hosts.

Dress is black tie

This Sunday also heralds the beginning of May Week. (The celebrations were originally held in May and the name has stuck despite the change of date.) This is the week when all the May Balls are held to end the year in the traditional style.

Just before May Week, college rowers have their final opportunity for sporting glory in the May Bumps (or 'Mays'). This is exactly the same as the Lent Bumps although it is always regarded as the more important event, and is certainly the one favoured by spectators who are happy to gather at the pubs along the river to watch. This, like the Lent Bumps, culminates in a college being crowned Head of the River and is celebrated by the traditional boat burning.

Famous for their extravagance, luxury and expense, May Balls are still regarded by most of the University's students as the high point of the year. The events take place in the grounds of the colleges and much preparation goes into the decorations, with lighting and flowers used to create a fairy tale atmosphere. Many Balls are themed; in recent years there has been 'Heaven and Hell', 'Seven Deadly Sins' and 'Alice in Wonderland'.

Cloister Court, Queens' College

Student protest outside King's

The Avenue, through the Backs to Trinity College

Great Court, Trinity College

All, however, contain the essential ingredients; champagne, fire-works and a number of bands to entertain the students in their lavish ball gowns or smart dinner jackets as they dance away the night. Most exam results are announced just after May Week and it is common to see crowds of students surrounding the screens outside the Senate House trying to see what their year's work amounted to. Grades at British universities are divided into four classes: first, upper second, lower second, and third. Most students are happy with either of the first two.

At the end of June the Senate House again becomes crowded as the setting for the graduation ceremonies. Graduands (those who are about to graduate) get dressed up in full academic robes – white bow ties, gowns and an 'ermine' hood. At the ceremony those receiving their degrees have to hold one of the Vice-Chancellor's fingers in groups of four, while he gives a Latin dec-laration.

This officially marks the end of the academic year, and for stu-dents returning for the next academic year it's off on the 'long vacation' until October.

At the ball

A Day In The Life Of The University

T here is no typical day in the life of a Cambridge student. Whilst a diligent science student may spend all day in lecture hall and library, a history student passionate about theatre may be spending all day and all night preparing for his or her production, putting off an essay to the last possible minute. It is for this reason that this section has been called 'A Day in the Life of the University' — it is an attempt to capture some of the different events going on amongst students in Cambridge.

Early morning rowing outing

5.30 am The first boat crews start to appear on the river Cam. It is difficult to find time to row, as students often have many commitments during the day, so some coaches ask their oarsmen or women to get up extremely early.

8.00 – 8.45 am Breakfast, either in their college's Hall (the cafeteria, often with a splendid dining room) or in students' rooms. Some students may be woken up by a knock on the door by their 'bedder', the room-cleaners traditionally employed by the colleges. Bedders have the right (and the keys) to enter students' rooms every morning except Sunday, and the traditional 'do not disturb' sign is to put one's waste bin outside the door. Bins outside doors are, naturally, the source of much gossip amongst neighbours, who may jump to conclusions as to just why someone does not wish to be disturbed.

9.00 am Lectures begin for the day. Most scientific courses, including medicine and veterinary medicine, require that their students attend a full day of lectures, sometimes seven hours' worth. Each lecture is one hour long. Arts faculties, such as those of History or English, put on lectures, but students are often much more selective about those which they attend. This is because there are usually fewer that are relevant to a particular student's chosen topics. Often, arts students will opt to spend the morning reading, either in the library or in their room, rather than go to a lecture.

1.00 pm Whilst lunch in Hall in the colleges will have started at around 12.30, one o'clock sees the second bicycle rush hour of the day (the first was at nine o'clock) as everybody returns from the lecture halls to find themselves something to eat.

2.00 pm Supervisions usually happen in the afternoon rather than the morning. As a student may have three or four a week, whatever subject (s)he does, they are a regular feature of life. Lectures, practicals and classes continue, for some, until six.

2.15 pm Inter-college sports matches are usually held in the afternoons. A wide range of sports are played, from netball to rugby union, and the contests are often hard-fought. Most colleges have their own sports grounds in and around the city.

5.45 pm – 7.00 pm Cafeteria dinner is available in Hall. A majority of students eat in Hall at some stage during the day, as it is usually the cheapest way of getting food.

7.30 pm Formal Hall starts. An occasion unique to Oxford and Cambridge, this was traditionally the smart dinner of the evening, a three-course waiter-served meal by candlelight . Now, Formal Hall is a smarter, longer and slightly more expensive alternative to cafeteria dinner, usually only chosen by students who have something to celebrate. Gowns must be worn to Formal Hall, but there are few other dress regulations, which often leads to the comic sight of a gown over jeans and T-shirt.

7.30 – 8.00 pm Student plays start at the Playroom in St. Edward's Passage and the ADC Theatre in Park Street, the oldest university playhouse in Britain. 'The ADC' is the centre of Cambridge's drama scene. Student plays are usually plentiful and of an extremely high quality, and sometimes written by undergraduates. Several Cambridge drama groups annually put on shows at the Edinburgh Fringe Festival, often to critical acclaim. The University has produced Emma Thompson, Oscar winning actress, and the celebrated director Sir Peter Hall, amongst others.

8.00 pm A concert may start at the University's West Road concert hall. Performances by the University Music Society (UMS) are usually the most accomplished, but individual and college groups often contain considerable talent.

8.15 pm Other University societies, from the Jewish Society to the Sports Parachuting Association, hold speaker meetings or get-togethers during the evening. The former can vary from the downright dull to the absorbingly interesting, whilst the latter are often held in pubs.

9.00 pm If it is a Friday or Saturday night, this is the time at which college discos, known as 'bops' or 'sweatys' start, although they never fill up until around eleven. Fitzwilliam College is well-known for its bi-termly 'Fitz Entz', often with well-known disc jockeys, and Trinity's 'Sweatys' are usually packed, serving cheap, ferocious cocktails such as 'Sex on the Backs'.

10.00 pm Again, if it is Friday or Saturday, undergraduate parties begin at this time. For some reason, private parties in Cambridge

Formal Hall at
Trinity Hall

never seem to start until ten, and reach a peak between midnight and one am. Parties can be held by entire staircases in a college, or by an individual. Theming of parties is popular, from 'tacos and tequila' to 'headgear essential'. Many an undergraduate's Friday or Saturday night is spent in regal progress from party to party and from college to college. Parties carry one wrinkle, however—permission usually has to be sought from the Senior Tutor or Lay Dean (the Fellows responsible for maintaining discipline) and many colleges' porters seem to take pride in shutting down illegal or over-long gatherings. Some invitations have been known to state '10 pm until the porters'.

10.15 pm College bars start to fill up, as students gather for a late-night drink after their evening's work or other activities. The bar is usually the social centre of the college, combined with the Junior Combination Room (always shortened to JCR, and traditional term for the undergraduates' common room). Most students can be sure of seeing their friends in one of these two places. Fellows have their own common rooms, the Senior Combination Rooms (SCRs), but in some colleges undergraduates, graduates and Fellows rub shoulders nightly at the bar. College bars vary enormously, but all rigorously maintain the rule of serving only college members and their guests.

11.00 pm Lateshows start at ADC and Playroom theatres. Often more avant-garde and risqué than the earlier 'mainshows', lateshows can vary from dance performances to productions of little-known plays. Footlights traditionally holds its bi-termly 'smokers' at this time in the ADC, comedy revues for which auditions, open to all comers, are held a few nights previously. Their standard is usually high.

2.00 am Those parties that are quiet or lucky enough not to have been 'busted' by the porters peter out, as everybody finds their way back to bed. Earlier in the century, students were obliged to be back in their rooms before a certain (early) time in the evening, or face severe penalties. Now, some colleges still maintain a system where 'late keys' must be signed out of the porters lodge to gain re-admission after a certain time.

3.00 am Those students who have delayed the writing of their essays to the last minute, or who simply have lots of work to do, can be found working into the small hours. 'Burning the midnight oil' due to what is known as an 'essay crisis' is something that most students will experience at some time.

(right) Student production of West Side Story

A Dictionary Of Cambridge Slang

A long way: anywhere more than five minutes' walk away.

Backs, *n*: the area between the backs of the colleges and Queens' Road, close to the Cam.

Bedder, *n*: Member of college staff (now always female) who makes students' beds and cleans their rooms.

Boatie, *n*: Rower, usually with same characteristics as a rugger-bugger.

Bop, a.k.a. **Sweaty**, a.k.a. **Event**, *n*: disco, sometimes with food, always with drink.

Ministry of Information or **UL**, *n*: The University Library.

Bumps, *n*: Complicated rowing races in which each college boat tries to catch up with the next.

'Cambridge' (as in 'so Cambridge'), *adj*: used to describe something that is meant to characterise student life, usually with sense of somebody taking something to extremes.

Cindy's: reference to 5th Avenue, nightclub, usually derogatory.

Compsci, *n*: Student reading computer science, usually derogatory. See natsci.

Confie, *n*: conference delegate (usually used in combination with irritation about 'how delegates take over colleges outside term'.)

Desmond (also dezzy), *n*: Lower second in exams, usually finals. From Desmond Tutu (two-two).

Dosser, *n*: Lazy person. (from 'doss-house').

Dweeb (rare), *n*: See narg.

Emma, n: Emmanuel College

Entz, *n(pl)*: Entertainments (usually provided by college JCRs).

Fitz, *n*: 1. Fitzwilliam College.
2. The ~ The Fitzwilliam Museum

Gardies, *n*: The Gardenia late-night takeaway, in Rose Crescent.

Grad-pad, *n*: The University Centre used by graduates for food and accommodation (from graduate + pad).

Gyp room, *n*: Small kitchen for student use, habitually with a few rings and no oven (from gyp, obsolete term for male bedder).

Hack, *n*: Excessively motivated, often selfish, student who attempts to get to the top of

undergraduate politics or journalism. Also to ~, *verb*.

JCR, *n*: Junior Combination Room. Either an undergraduate common room, or the students elected to look after undergraduate affairs by their peers.

King Street Run, *n*: Tour of the King St pubs in each of which the participants must drink a pint.

Mathmo, *n*: Student reading Mathematics.

May Week, *n*: Week in June (confusingly) when May Balls occur. (f. original month when balls were held.)

Muso, *n*: 1. Student reading music.
2. Musician (often one and the same).

Narg, *n*: A student (usually male) who is hard-working, boring and socially inept; typically physically unattractive and badly-dressed. 2, *v.i.* To ~ (perh. f. imitating narg's manner of speech).

Natsci, *n*: student of natural sciences, usually derogatory, hinting that they are nargs.

Pidge or P/hole, *n*: student's mail pigeon-hole (abbrev.)

Plodge, *n*: porters' lodge (abbrev.)

Quiche, *v.i.*: to wimp out, to be cowardly and weak.

Rag, *n*: students' fund-raising charity. Also ~ Week. (f. obs. Rag=jape)

Rugger-bugger, *n*: Rugby-player, esp. one given to rowdy behaviour and drunkenness.

Shark, *v.t.*: to pursue members of the opposite sex unscrupulously.

Spod, *n*: See narg.

Squash, *n*: open meeting at start of year (usually alcoholic) of a college or University society for the purposes of recruiting new members.

Thesp, 1, *n*: student actor or actress, usually with associated pretentiousness and tendency to show off. 2. *v.i.* to act 3. *v.i.* to behave in a thespy (*adj*) manner.

Tit Hall, *n*: Trinity Hall (abbrev.)

Trash, *v.t.*: to ransack a room or divest it of its contents, usu. after party.

Typewriter, *n*: Christ's College New Court (f. its shape).

Vac, *n*: vacation. (abbrev.)

Guided

Tours

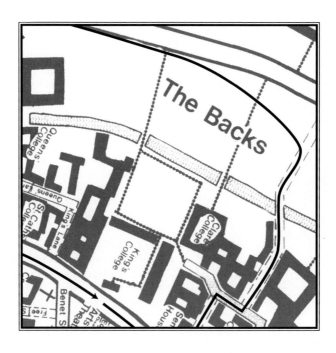

Walk One:
The Riverside Colleges

Facing King's College Porters' Lodge, turn right along King's Parade. Just after King's College Chapel on your left, you will see a large neo-classical building, the Senate House, and opposite it on the right, Great St Mary's Church (p 64).

A large University assembly hall, the Senate House fulfils a number of functions, most importantly as an examination hall and as the place where degrees are given out at the end of a student's time at Cambridge. The boards ouside the Senate House are covered with sheets of examination results towards the end of the Easter term (end of May – beginning of June).

The Senate House was the scene of the most famous undergraduate joke derived from the sport of 'night-climbing' amidst the roofs of Cambridge. On one occasion in June 1958, the city awoke to find an old Austin van sitting on the roof of the Senate House. This feat was most recently matched by those who managed to scale King's Chapel one night and fix a banner 38 feet long reading "Peace in Vietnam" between the towers facing King's Parade. The climbers responsible for this feat were later caught by the police after climbing onto the Senate House roof, and 'sent down' (expelled from the University).

Go through the traffic barriers into a cobbled area, with the Senate House on your left. In front of you is Gonville and Caius College (p 16), always shortened to just 'Caius' (pronounced 'keys', the latinised version of the name of the co-founder, Dr. John Keys). Veer to the left and turn down a small cobbled alley, Senate House Pasage, keeping the Senate House on your left. Follow this alley to the end.

**Caius College Gate
of Honour**

As you pass down the alley, notice the elaborate gate on your right. This is Caius' Gate of Honour, crowned by sundials, and made to an Italian model. It is the third of the three gates which a student at Caius would go through in his time at the college, as designed by Dr. John Keys. The others were the Gates of Humility and Virtue.

At the end of Senate House Passage, you will notice an alley to the left. If you go down here, you will come to Clare College (p 15) on your right, and the visitors' entrance to King's College Chapel.

If you wish to carry on with the route of this walk, however, turn right at the end of Senate House Passage, passing the entrance to Trinity Hall (p 16) on the left. Shortly afterwards, turn left again down Garret

(right) King's College Porters' Lodge

Hostel Lane. There should be 'To The River' marked in chalk on one of the walls of this lane, with an arrow pointing down it.

Follow this lane over the steep Garret Hostel Bridge; before it reaches a large main road (Queens' Road), you will notice two parallel paths off to the left. Take the first of these paths, keeping the trees and the road to your right. You are now on Cambridge's famous Backs (you can see the backs of the colleges from this area). Carry on along the Backs until you see the splendour of King's College over a field to your left. If you see people without feet, but standing up holding poles, moving slowly but regularly along in front of the lawns next to the chapel, you are not hallucinating — they are punting!

The path will end in a line of barriers just after you see King's Chapel, and you will notice the back entrance to the college on your left. The path has led you onto the pavement beside Queens' Road.

There are two small crests on the gate, one with three roses in the bottom half of the shield, and another with three fleur de lis. The crest with the roses on is that of King's; the one to the right of it, with the lilies, is that of Eton College, the famous English public school. King's and Eton were founded to complement each other – Eton scholars were supposed to continue their education at the college.

Go through or around the barriers and take the footpath which crosses the green space diagonally to the left of you. (If this is a problem for wheelchairs, follow Queens' Road and take the first left down Silver Street, following the instructions from the next paragraph.) Follow this path until you reach the barriers at the end, and then turn left onto Silver Street.

**Queens' College
Mathematical
Bridge**

Follow Silver Street over the Cam. As you pass over the bridge, look to your left, and you will see Queens' famous Mathematical Bridge. One apocryphal student story relates that the bridge would stand up on its own without the bolts holding the bridge's beams to each other, but undergraduates were so adept at taking it apart that it had to be fixed together!

Shortly after you have crossed the river, you will see Queens' Lane off to your left, which leads to the visitors' entrance to Queens' College. If you are not visiting Queens', carry on up Silver Street until it turns sharply to the right into Trumpington Street, next to Ede and Ravenscroft, the gentleman's outfitter's shop on the corner.

At this junction, turn left into Trumpington Street. You will pass St Catharine's College on your left, and Corpus Christi College on your right. Follow this road until you see King's Porters' Lodge on your left.

Walk Two: Central Colleges

The front of Emmanuel College

Facing King's College Porter's Lodge, turn left along King's Parade. Carry on straight ahead as it turns into Trumpington Street opposite No 1 King's Parade Restaurant. You will pass Corpus Christi College on your left and St Catharine's College on your right. Soon, you will reach a junction, with St Benet's church on your left (p 63).

At the junction, carry on along the left side of Trumpington Street for a few metres, until you see St Botolph's Lane off to the left. Follow this small road to its end. Next, veer right and you will reach Pembroke Street. Turn left, and follow this road right to its end at a T-junction and traffic lights. You will find that its name changes to Downing Street after 20 metres or so.

When you reach the end of this road, you will see a large classical entrance over the road in front of you. This is Emmanuel College, famous for its former student John Harvard, founder of the Massachusetts university, and, amongst contemporary University students, for its ducks (see p21). Turn left at the T-junction into St Andrew's Street. When the road bends around to the right, carry on straight ahead over the cobbles, following St Andrew's Street. After a while, the road will fork, and you will see an ornate gatehouse on the right. This is the entrance to Christ's College (p 21). Take the left-hand fork.

You will notice that you are either passing through or going around a set of gates. These, and the various other traffic obstacles that you will see at certain junctions around the city, are part of Cambridge City Council's controversial scheme which bans bicycles and traffic from the centre of town. Most spectacular are the obstacles which rise from and descend into the road to allow particular vehicles access to the restricted area. Follow Sidney Street as it bends slightly to the right. When Market Street joins from the left just after the branch of Woolworth's, carry on straight ahead along Sidney Street. About 40 metres or so along this road you will see a college gate to your right and Sainsbury's supermarket opposite, on your left.

The college on your right is Sidney Sussex college, sometimes known to students as 'Sidney Sainsbury's', because of its proximity to the supermarket. Perhaps fed-up with this nickname,

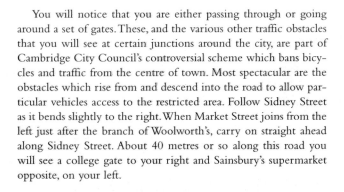

(right) Trinity College Great Gate

students from the college once painted a pedestrian crossing across Sidney Street from the entrance of their college to the entrance of Sainsbury's, and proceeded to use it until it was removed.

When Sidney Street reaches a junction go straight on into Bridge Street ahead of you. After 40 metres or so, you will see church on your right. This is The Round Church (the origin of its name is self-evident). See page 64 for more details.

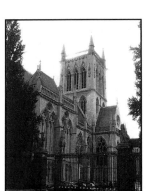

St John's College Chapel

To the right of the Round Church as you face it you will see a small alleyway, and a notice which shows the way to the Cambridge Union Society. One of the largest and oldest student societies (it was founded in 1815), it provides a forum for political and social debate. 'The Union', as it is known, still attracts many politicians and personalities to speak at its weekly debates.

The tradition of Union politics is so strong that it has been suggested that there is something of a 'Cambridge Mafia' in the British Conservative Party today. Carry on a little way along Bridge Street until St John's Street branches off to your left. Turn into St John's Street. On your right, you will notice the immense edifice of St John's College Chapel, and further along, the entrance to the College (p 18). Carry on along St John's Street and you will come to Trinity College Great Gate, again on your right.

If you look up at the statue of Henry VIII, founder of the college, in the centre of the gate, you will notice that he is not holding a sceptre in his right hand, but a chair-leg. This is testimony to the dangerous undergraduate sport of night-climbing, the scaling of university buildings under the cover of darkness. Some time in the early nineteenth century, when it was the fashion for fellows to wear wigs, the barber serving Trinity was bribed by undergraduates to climb up the college Library and put the best wigs belonging to the Senior Fellows on the head of the statues facing the Hall.

Continue along the same street, which has now become Trinity Street. You will pass Heffers, the city's most encyclopaedic bookshop, on your left, and some way further along, Gonville and Caius (pronounced 'keys') College on your right (p 16). Carry on along Trinity Street until you see King's College Chapel over to the right as you reach the junction with St Mary's Street. Cross over the road, through the barriers, and head up King's Parade, remaining on the left side of the road.

Carry on along King's Parade, and you will find yourself at King's College Porter's Lodge once more.

Walk Three: Grantchester Meadows

Grantchester, with its winding streets and thatched roofs, has long been a retreat for students. Just far enough out of Cambridge to feel 'away', undergraduates take to the village for a quiet drink in one of the pubs, as a destination for a long punting trip, or purely to see some countryside. The village's name is derived from the Cam's other name, the 'Granta'. The poet Rupert Brooke nostagically recalled the two years (1910-1912) he spent in the 17th-century Old Vicarage in his well-known poem *Grantchester*, and the house is now home to the popular novelist Jeffrey Archer.

The Orchard Tea Gardens is an excellent place to stop and rest once you have reached Grantchester. Wittgenstein, Virginia Woolf and John Maynard Keynes have taken tea amongst the trees here, and its bohemian atmosphere and comfortable deck-chairs are ideal for relaxation on a fine summers' day (inside seating is available when the weather is unkind). The Tea Garden is, sadly, in danger through debt and developers; hopefully, it will survive during the lifetime of this guidebook.

The Mill Pub

If you are in search of stronger refreshment, Grantchester boasts three good pubs; The Green Man, The Red Lion, and The Rupert Brooke, all of which also serve food. The best views are available from The Rupert Brooke. All three pubs are on the route of the walk below. This walk takes the visitor to the village the classic way, through Grantchester Meadows beside the Cam. Facing King's Porter's Lodge, turn left and follow King's Parade and Trumpington Street to the junction with Silver Street, just by St Botolph's church. On your way, you will pass St Catharine's College on your right and Corpus Christi College on your left.

Keep going straight ahead over the junction, crossing onto the right side of the road, where you will see a large Gothic building. This is the old site of the Cambridge University Press, now the Pitt Building. Walking to the far end of this building you will come to Mill Lane on your right. Follow Mill Lane past the University Careers Service and the Department of Pure Maths until you reach the Mill Pub, a favourite with students in the summer when they have finished their exams.

Opposite the pub you will see a gate and bridge over the Cam. Cross the river and follow the path beside it, which veers to the left When the path forks, take the right-hand path. Walk across two

(right) Grantchester Meadows

bridges, reaching a junction of paths. Take the left-hand path alongside a stream on the right. Cross the main road and continue across the green, named Lammas Land, on the path in front of you until you come to another main road. Turn left along this road and carry on straight ahead into Granchester Street close by.

Follow Granchester Street until you reach the third road on the right, Eltisley Avenue. Go to the end, then take the road straight in front of you which veers slightly to the right. Carry on into a gravelled car park, following the Public Footpath sign to Granchester. At the end of the car park, take a narrow hedged byway which leads to Granchester Meadows through a gate. Follow the long tarmac path through the meadows through three more gates.

Carry on straight ahead through another gate until you reach a main road. You have reached Grantchester. The Orchard Tea Garden, an excellent place to stop and have a cool drink, is a little way along the road to the left. To carry on with the main walk, turn right at the main road and continue until you reach the Green Man pub and a small village green. The Red Lion is a little further along the small road to the right, past the Green Man. At this point, the disabled will need to retrace their journey to return to Cambridge.

**The Green Man
Pub, Grantchester**

Carry on along the main road until you reach the Rupert Brooke pub on the right. Go to the extreme left-hand end of the pub's garden and car park and you will find a stile back into the meadows. Head straight ahead across the meadow until you reach the path once more. Turn left onto the path and retrace your steps as far as the city centre end of Granchester Street.

At this point, take the road to your right, at right-angles to Grantchester Street, with yellow lines along it. It is signposted 'The Granta Housing Trust'. Follow this road until you see an entrance to a car park on your right. Take the path in front of you through the barriers and over a black bridge. Carry on, veering slightly left along the path until you come to a junction of paths just before a boathouse. Take the left-hand path around the boathouse and continue alongside the river until you reach the main road.

Cross the road and turn right onto the pavement. Carry on along this road until you reach a set of roundabouts. Turn left at the first roundabout and the carry straight on along Trumpington Street. Follow Trumpington Street, passing the Fitzwilliam Museum, Peterhouse and Pembroke, until you reach the Pitt building once more. Retrace your steps along Trumpington Street and King's Parade to King's Porter's Lodge.

Walk Four:
Jesus, Magdelene and
Open Spaces

Facing King's Porter's Lodge, turn right along King's Parade. Soon, you will notice Great St. Mary's Church, the University Church, on your right (see p 63). Just after Great St. Mary's, go through the traffic barriers and turn left down Market Street. Carry on down Market Street, passing Cambridge's Market on your right.

Market Street veers sharply to the left close to the stationery department of Heffers. Follow the road round. Its name will change to Sidney Street, but carry on straight ahead, past Sidney Sussex college on your right (p 21) and the branch of Sainsbury's supermarket opposite. Soon after you have passed the entrance to Sidney Sussex, Sidney Street will come to the point at which a road comes in from the right and continues straight ahead.

Turn right down the road coming in from the right, Jesus Lane, crossing onto the left side of the road. Carry on along Jesus Lane until you reach some traffic lights.m On your left, is the ADC Theatre. The home of Cambridge's flourishing student drama scene, it shows two plays a week during term-time. Student actors and actresses at Cambridge are known as 'Thesps' (from thespian), and are caricatured amongst undergraduates as insincere and exhibitionist. Nevertheless, Cambridge theatre is usually of a very high quality, and the ADC is definitely worth a visit.

Cross straight over the road and the traffic lights, and carry on along the left side of Jesus Lane for about 300 metres. Opposite the tall spire of the church on the right hand side of the road, you will notice a black wrought-iron gate to your left, and a long walled passage behind it. Wesley House. This is the entrance to Jesus College (p 20). The walkway is known as 'the chimney'.

If you are not visiting Jesus, carry on along Jesus lane another 200 metres until you reach a roundabout. Keeping to the left-hand side of the road, follow the pavement as it turns along Victoria Avenue, the first turning to the left out of the roundabout. Continue straight along this avenue of trees for about 300 metres, until you reach a pedestrian crossing where the road bends.

As you pass along Victoria Avenue, notice the green space to your right, on the other side of the road. This is Midsummer Common,

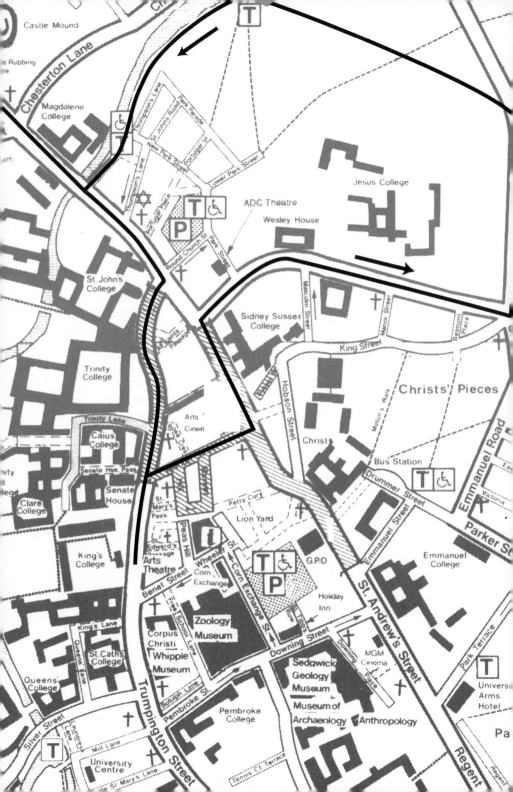

where a fair has been held since. The buildings on the far side of the common are college and university boathouses.

At the pedestrian crossing, turn left through some metal barriers onto a path across a park in front of you, Jesus Green. The path is another avenue of trees. Carry on straight ahead down the avenue, ignoring the path which crosses it half-way across Jesus Green, until you reach a bridge over the Cam and a lock. Turn left onto the path which follows the left bank of the Cam. After fifty or so metres, the path forks, with the tarmac veering off to the left and another path turning right, through some barriers, and keeping close to the Cam.

Take the right-hand path, keeping the Spade and Becket pub to your left, and moving onto a wooden walkway. Follow the walkway and the Cam until you reach Magdelene Bridge and Bridge Street.

If you wish to visit Magdelene College, or climb up Castle Mound, then turn right over Magdelene Bridge into Magdelene Street. About 30 metres along Magdelene Street, to the right as you go up it, is the entrance to Magdelene College (p 20). To get to Castle Mound, carry on up Magdelene Street. At the traffic lights, carry on straight up Castle Hill, on the right hand side of the road. After you pass the Castle Inn you will see a small path to the right. Take this path, which crosses the car park of Shire Hall, the large building to the left (the headquarters of Cambridgeshire County Council.) On the right, you will see Castle Mound and the path which leads up to it. Retrace your steps and carry on back over Magdelene Bridge onto Bridge Street. Ignore the next paragraph, and then follow the remainder of the walk back to King's.

If you wish to return to King's Parade, turn left at Magdalene Bridge, down Bridge Street.

Follow this road until you see St. John's Street off to the right, then turn into it.. On your right, you will notice the immense edifice of St. John's College chapel, and further along, the entrance to the college (p 18). Carry on along St John's Street and you will come to Trinity College on your right (p 16).

Continue along the same street, which has now become Trinity Street. You will pass Heffers, the city's most encyclopaedic bookshop, on your left, and some way further along, Gonville and Caius (pronounced "keys") College on your right (p 16). Carry on along Trinity Street until you see King's College Chapel over to the right as you reach the junction with St. Mary's Street. Cross over the road, through the barriers, and head up King's Parade, remaining on the left side of the road.

Carry on along King's Parade, and you will find yourself at King's College Porters' Lodge once more.

By The River

Walking is not the only way to see the beauty of Cambridge. In fact, on a hot summer's day there is no better way to view the colleges that line the Backs than drifting along in a punt.

Punting is the quintessence of the Cambridge myth – a handsome young man wearing boater and blazer guides his craft below the eight bridges, with a beautiful woman smiling up at him as he glides down the Cam. The picture almost holds true today, although blazer and boater have given way to T-shirt and baseball cap – punting still remains one of the favourite ways for the Cambridge undergraduate to relax.

While most colleges don't hire their punts out to the public, it is possible for the visitor to hire a punt for the day or by the hour, with or without the services of an experienced punt-chauffeur, from one of the punt-hire companies operating along the river.

Punt-chauffeur services may offer anything from a full day's outing, complete with packed hamper and expert commentary on the sights, to little more than a competent hand on the pole. The more adventurous or athletic, however, may hire a punt by the hour from any of the jetties along the river, and do the driving for themselves.

Lesson one – how to punt

Before you start, there are one or two preparations you can make. Don't wear clothing that could be stained by river water. While punts are extremely difficult to capsize, it is very easy to fall out of one, especially if you are standing up. In addition, when handling the pole, water tends to run down your arm, so it is best to roll up your sleeves. Do wear shoes with good grips – if you have smooth soles, bare feet are probably a better bet.

Always stand squarely on the platform at the rear of the punt. If you feel insecure there, you can stand in the well behind the seats, thought this makes the punt harder to control. Try not to stand towards one side of the punt, as this will make it lean alarmingly.

The main problems that newcomers to punting face tend to centre around using the pole correctly. Hold the pole vertical

directly at your side, with the end just above the water. Let it slip fast through your fingers, so that it hits the river bed. Holding with both hands, push downwards on the pole so that it tilts forwards. Make sure that the pole moves parallel to the punt – if it tilts at an angle, the punt will move to the side and swing round. If this happens, don't panic. Hold the pole so that it drags in the water behind the punt. Holding it at a shallow angle, half way out of the water, with your bottom hand quite low down the pole, use the pole as a rudder. If you point the pole to the left, the punt will move to the left, and vice versa. Once you're on course, pull the pole up and let it down as before, repeating the stroke to build up speed.

When you're on the move, beware of a few notorious pitfalls:

• Don't attempt to get in a stroke before a bridge unless there are at least two full lengths of a punt in front of you. Poles are long things, and when they get jammed between the arch of a bridge and a river bed, you're in for trouble.

• Don't be tempted to hold onto the pole if it gets stuck in the river bed or against a bridge. Poles float, and can be retrieved by paddling back. If you hold on, the punt will drift onwards and you will slide off, clutching the pole. If you feel the pole sticking, twist it as you pull, but if it stays stuck, let it go!

• Beware of the deep areas under Magdalene Bridge (it's the big cast-iron road bridge next to Magdalene and St John's Colleges). The river there is deeper than the length of some poles, so hang onto yours and just drift through.

Where to go

There are two classic punting routes in Cambridge. The first is from Magdalene Bridge to Silver Street Bridge. This lasts about an hour, and takes you along the famous backs of the colleges, beneath all the bridges in the city centre. Especially beautiful is the stretch between St John's Bridge of Sighs and Queens' Mathematical Bridge.

The other route is up-river from Silver Street to the delightful village of Grantchester. This lasts an afternoon and takes you through Grantchester Meadows, made famous by Rupert Brooke; you can moor at the bank there and picnic in pleasant surroundings, or buy a drink at one of the nearby pubs.

(left) The Cam

Punt companies

A ll punt companies require a deposit on hire punts. Chauffeur punt trips vary in length, between 40 minutes and an hour for going along the backs, and are longer (and dearer) for going up river towards Grantchester.

CAMBRIDGE PUNT COMPANY
Anchor Pub
Tel: 01223 357565

TRINITY COLLEGE PUNT HIRE
Garret Hostel Lane
Tel: 01223 338483

GRANTA PUNT COMPANY
Granta Pub, Newnham Road
Tel: 01223 301845

TYRRELLS MARINE
Quayside
Trips are negotiable for big parties.
Tel: 01223 363080

SCUDAMORES
Quayside (Magdalene Bridge) and two at Mill Lane (by the Mill Pub).
Tel: 01223 359750 (hire punts) 01223 321697 (chauffeur punts)
Punts from Quayside are only available for use on the Backs.
Chauffered punts, guided tours and picnics can be arranged.

Where
To Go

Where To Go

C ambridge has a lot to offer beyond the confines of the college courts. The city has a long and complex history of its own, and this is reflected in the enormous variety of buildings and its twisting mediaeval passageways and lanes. There is much to do and see around Cambridge. Here is a selection of the essentials.

Approximate times of University terms:

Michaelmas	Early October - early December
Lent	Late January - mid March
Easter	Late April - early June

Guided Tours

The best way for big groups to see the major sights is by taking a guided tour with one of the registered blue-badged guide, as many of the big colleges require large groups to be accompanied. Go to the Tourist Information Centre to sign up.

Bus Tours

Tickets and information from Guide Friday, Cambridge Railway Station. Telephone (01223) 362444

Tours of the city, taking in the American Cemetery at Madingley, run regularly; every 10 - 15 minutes in the summer, every 20 minutes in the spring and autumn, and every hour in the winter months. Bus tours, which include a commentary on the sights, are a good way for a visitor in a hurry to see the city.

Walking Tours

Tickets and information from the Tourist Information Centre, Wheeler Street. Telephone (01223) 322640

Tours go very regularly in the summer, and twice daily in the winter months, departing from the Information Centre. They include visits to college grounds, with an informed commentary from a trained guide.

Museums and Galleries

A s a great seat of learning, the University runs several musuems for the benefit of its students. In addition, there are a number of museums and exhibitions charting the development of the city, and several excellent galleries. All information is subject to change.

THE CAMBRIDGE AND COUNTY FOLK MUSEUM
2 Castle Street
Tel: (01223) 355159
The Folk Museum inhabits what was once an inn called 'The White Horse'. It is crammed with artefacts from Cambridge and the surrounding area, all of which would have been used in daily life during the past few hundred years. Exhibits include an entire 18th century shop front, and the standard weights and measures dating from the time when the University ruled the city.

THE CAMBRIDGE DARKROOM
Dales Brewery, Gwydir Street
Tel: (01223) 350275
Admission free
As its name suggests, the Cambridge Darkroom speciaslises in photography as an art form. Its aim is to encourage new artists, and it achieves this with an accessibility to be envied by larger and longer-established rivals. The Darkroom also runs talks and photographic workshops throughout the year, and provides darkroom facilities for amateur photographers.

Lions guard the Fitz museum

KETTLE'S YARD
Northampton Street
Tel: (01223) 352124
Admission free
Kettle's Yard is a unique collection of modern sculptures, paintings and drawings, donated to the University by Jim Ede in 1966, complete with the house. Attached to the house is a gallery which ususally exhibits modern art or craft works.

THE FITZWILLIAM MUSEUM
Trumpington Street
Tel: (01223) 332900
Admisssion free
'The Fitz' is the University's art museum, and dates from 1816. The building is the work of George Basevi, who died before it was completed. The original collections of the founder, the seventh Viscount Fitzwilliam, have grown over the years. They now range from Egyptian, Greek and Roman antiquities to paintings by the French Impressionists. The library ranges from illuminated manuscripts to lit-

literary curios such as the first draft of Keats' *Ode to a Nightingale*. Works on display include Rembrandt's *Portrait of a Man* and Titian's *Venus and Cupid with a Lute Player*. The Upper Galleries are mainly given over to paintings, the lower to antiquities.

THE MUSEUM OF CLASSICAL ARCHAEOLOGY
Sidgwick Avenue
Tel: (01223) 335155
Admission free
This museum, housed in the Department of Classics, boasts a collection of more than 500 casts of Greek and Roman sculptures, reliefs and statues. The museum is very much a working one, with exhibits clearly displayed to aid study.

THE SCOTT POLAR RESEARCH MUSEUM
Lensfield Road
Tel: (01223) 336540
Admission free
The Scott Polar Research Institute is a memorial to the Antartic explorer Captain Scott and his companions, who died during the epic race to reach the South Pole. On display are relics from his expeditions – including a sledge and eskimo artefacts – and exhibits explaining current polar research.

THE UNIVERSITY MUSEUM OF ARHCAEOLOGY AND ANTHROPOLOGY
Downing Street
Admission free, but donations welcome
The multitude of exhibits spans the globe, representing American, African, Pacific and South-East Asian cultures as well as covering the Cambridge area.

THE UNIVERSITY MUSEUM OF ZOOLOGY
New Museums Site, Downing Street
Admission free
A collection representing the whole spectrum of animal life. Exhibits include fossils of now-extinct species, as well as preserved mammals, birds, insects and marine life.

THE WHIPPLE MUSEUM OF THE HISTORY OF SCIENCE
Free School Lane
Admission free
The museum is based on a collection of scientific instruments amassed by R S Whipple, which was given to the University in 1944. On display are many fascinating devices, inlcuding a clock work model of the solar system dating from around 1750, early surveying instruments, microscopes and telescopes, and electrostatic generators.

THE SEDGWICK MUSEUM OF GEOLOGY
Downing Site, Downing Street
Tel: (01223) 333456
Admission free
Based on the collection of fossils started by Adam Sedgwick
(Woodwardian proffessor of Geology until 1873), this well-organ-
ised museum sports the skeleton of an iguanadon, an Irish elk and
an hippopotamus – the latter excavated at Barrington, near
Cambridge. The museum also houses the oldest intact geological
collection in the world, gathered by Dr John Woodward (1665-
1738), and boasts a fossil of the largest spider ever found – 36cm
across.

Churches

Cambridge has many picturesque and ancient churches which are
well worth visiting. A few are as old as the city itself, and many
are remarkably beautiful.

ST BENE'T'S CHURCH (ST BENEDICT'S)
Bene't Street
St Bene't's Saxon tower is the oldest building in Cambridge. It
was probably built around 1025, while the nave was rebuilt in the
13th century. Other parts were added in the 14th and 15th centuries, including the gallery connecting the church with neighbouring Corpus Christi College. St. Bene't's served as Corpus'
Chapel for over 300 years.

**Bene't Street
Church**

ST EDWARD, KING AND MARTYR
St Edward's Passage
This church, tucked away behind King's Parade, is dedicated to
the Saxon king, Edward the Confessor. Most of the building dates
from the 15th century, although the tower is probably 12th century. The aisles were built around 1450 by Trinity Hall and Clare
Hall, to serve as college chapels after their local church was pulled
down to make way for King's College.

LITTLE ST MARY'S CHURCH
Trumpington Street
The church was originally dedicated to St. Peter, and acted as
chapel for Peterhouse until 1632. It was rebuilt and re-dedicated
to the Virgin Mary in 1350. Near the entrance is a memorial to
Godfrey Washington, who died in 1729, a fellow of Peterhouse
and relative of George Washington. The memorial includes the
Washington crest of three stars and stripes surmounted by an
eagle, which was the basis for the flag of the United States
of America.

View of the city from
Great St Mary's
Church Tower

GREAT ST MARY'S, THE UNIVERSITY CHURCH
King's Parade
The present church was built in 1478 to replace an earlier 14th century one. Formerly known as 'St Mary's by the Market', it is still used for some University ceremonies, and the University sermon is preached there every Sunday evening during term. The church is also the starting-point from which the first milestones in Britain were measured: undergraduates are still required to live within three miles of it in order to count 'in residence'. If nine terms are not spent within these boundaries, then the student cannot graduate. The tower of the church, which was built in 1608, is usually open to the public, and provide panoramic views over the city.

THE ROUND CHURCH (HOLY SEPULCHRE CHURCH)
Round Church Street
One of Cambridge's most popular tourist sites, this is one of the very few churches in Britain to be built with a circular nave, in commemoration of the Holy Sepulchre in Jerusalem. It was erected in 1130, and the chancel and north aisle were rebuilt in the 15th century. The present roof is a 19th century replacement for the original 15th-century polygonal bell-tower, which was removed during the course of restoration work carried out by Anthony Salvin in 1841.

Parks and Gardens

T here are many lovely open spaces around the city centre. **Jesus Green**, between Jesus College and the Cam (access from Bridge Street, Chesterton and Victoria) is the largest and offers a delightful riverside walk and is an ideal spot for picnics. Just across Victoria Avenue is **Midsummer Common**, where the city's spectacular Guy Fawkes Night fireworks display is held every November. The Midsummer Fair, held annually on the common, has roots in mediaeval times. **Parker's Piece** is cynically known as 'reality checkpoint' as it is felt that this marks the south-eastern boundary between Town and Gown.

Sheep's Green (access by the bridge at the end of Mill Lane) is a favourite place to stop and picnic, as it is right next to the Mill Pub, and close to the river. **Lammas Land** is a little further along the towpath and can be a little quieter during the summer. A little further afield are the wide expanses of **Grantchester Meadows** (see the Walks section).

It should be noted that colleges discourage picnickers in their grounds. However there are grassy areas along the Backs that lend

(right) Midsummer Common

Down by the Cam

The 1996 ADC and Footlights production of *Sleeping Beauty*

The Varsity Match

The May Bumps – chaos on the Cam

themselves to a pleasant break from the bustle of the centre of town. At the end of the summer term some colleges' Fellows' Gardens are open to the public under the National Gardens Scheme.

The University Botanic Gardens consists of 40 acres of gardens, delightfully laid out, with a variety of lawns, flower beds, plant houses and an eye-catching rockery. The collections are second only to those at Kew in botanic importance, and this is an excellent place to relax. Entrances can be found on Hills Road, Trumpington Street and Bateman Street.

The Theatre

A side from various in-college theatre stages, Cambridge has four main external drama venues. Most well-known, and the home of the Footlights, is the **ADC Theatre** on Park Street, for which ticket bookings can be made at the Arts Cinema box office (Tel: (01223) 504444). Aside from being the central venue for student theatre, the ADC also runs film seasons, especially during the examination period in the middle of Easter Term. **The Arts Theatre**, on Peas Hill (just off Market Square), has just re-opened following three years of renovation work and handles mostly external touring companies. Its repertoire is varied, and also encompasses opera, dance and musicals. The box office is open from 10am Mon-Sat (Tel: (01223) 503333). **The Playroom** in St Edward's Passage is also popular for student drama, tickets are sold on the door. **The Cambridge Drama Centre**, off Mill Road, also offers a wide range of plays as well as learning and experimental workshops, with tickets available on the door (Tel: (01223) 322748). **The Junction**, off Clifton Road, also stages dance and theatre (*Tel: (01223) 412600*).

A dance show at the Arts Theatre

The Cinema

C ambridge has three cinemas, the **ABC** on St Andrews Street, (*Tel: (01223) 364537*) the **Arts Cinema** in Market Passage (*Tel: (01223) 5044444*), and further out, the multi-screen **Warner Bros** in the Grafton Centre (*Tel: (01223) 460411*) . The ABC has two screens and shows films on general release, the programme changing every Friday. It also screens late shows, so there are usually up to four films to chose from, though there is no advance booking. The Arts Cinema caters for the enthusiast, with continental and less 'mainstream' fims shown every week. During the summer it hosts the Cambridge Film Festival. Its monthly programme is available from the box office or from the Tourist

(right) Student production of *Patience*

Information Centre in Wheeler Street. Tickets can be purchased in advance from the box office. Warner Bros show general release films and offer a telephone booking service.

Music

The musical repertoire of Cambridge is wide and varied. For the jazz enthusiast the **Anchor Pub** on Silver Street has a jazz night on Tuesdays, the **Bun Shop** on King Street has occasional jazz nights and the **Junction** has a Modern Jazz Club. **The Old Orleans** restaurant on Mill Lane also features jazz on occasion, and the **Boat Race Pub**, on Burleigh Street in the Grafton Centre, has a varied selection of bands 7 nights a week, *Tel: (01223) 360873*.

For the classically inclined, the **University Music Society** performs orchestral and choral works regularly at the University's West Road Concert Hall. The best way to find out what is being performed by college-based orchestral groups is to ask at Porters' Lodges. Perhaps the most well-known is **King's College Chapel Choir**, who can be heard during services in the College Chapel. Contact the Porter's Lodge at King's for details on 350411. The most versatile, all-round venue for music in Cambridge is **the Corn Exchange** in Wheeler Street, *Tel: (01223) 335781*, behind the Market Square, which has in the past attracted artists from the Bolshoi Ballet to the Manic Street Preachers. Tickets are best booked in advance from the box office.

Night Clubs

For those who can do without a night's sleep, there are two night-clubs in the centre of town. **The Q Club** on Wheeler Street offers a variety of different styles of music depending on which night you choose. More conventional is **5th Avenue**, *Tel: (01223) 364222,* in Lion Yard, open every night until 2am. **The Junction**, *Tel: (01223) 412600*, also holds specialised discos which are advertised in its monthly programme. Tickets can be purchased in advance from the Junction box office or from the Arts Cinema. **The Corn Exchange**, on Wheeler Street, *Tel: (01223) 335781*, also has occasional all-night dance events. Contact the box office for details.

In Summer

Cambridge City Council traditionally organised the Cambridge Festival in July, but that has now been replaced by a whole summer of events entitled 'Summer in the City', featuring street theatre to drive-in movies and ice skating.

July's other annual events remain, however, including the Fringe, a theatre festival organised by the ADC Theatre; the Film Festival, hosted by the Arts Cinema; and the Folk Festival, traditionally held in the grounds of Cherry Hinton Hall. Contact the Tourist Information Centre or the relevant venues for more details.

Shopping

The National Trust Shop

T he most interesting shops in Cambridge are clustered in the historic city centre, within the ring of the older colleges. With shops selling everything from books to blazers and gifts to gowns, no visitors should have any problems finding suitable souvenirs of their stay in Cambridge.

Edible purchases are easily available. **The National Trust Shop**, on King's Parade, sells a variety of biscuits and jams, and **Bellina**, on All Saint's Passage, sells a mouth-watering array of chocolates. **Fitzbillies**, in Trumpington Street, even post their famous Chelsea Buns worldwide. **Jim Garrahy's Fudge Kitchen** on King's Parade is the place to buy hand made gudge in an array of flavours, or even to watch one of the frequent fudge making demonstrations.

There is no shortage of novelty gift shops in the town. The aptly-named **Choice**, in Rose Crescent, is home to a bewildering plethora of gifts, including chess men shaped like fellows. Alternatively, gift ideas are in plentiful supply at **WOW** (also in Rose Crescent). For the wealthier shopper there are a number of imaginative jewellers, including **Catherine Jones** on Bridge St and **Cellini** (Rose Crescent) For the bored executive, **Chaps** in Green St is a must; a wealth of executive toys guaranteed to keep even the most active mind amused for hours lurks within the door. Just next door is **Past Times**, which sells everything from tapestries to board games, all with an historical theme. For that extra cuddly present a visit to **The English Teddy Bear Company** on King's Parade, is a must; this cosy shop specialises in teddy bears of all shapes and sizes, every one of them crying out to be taken home!

As you might expect from a university town, Cambridge has more than its fair share of bookshops. Most famous of all is **Heffers**, the official University booksellers, which has customers throughout the world. Their main bookshop is on Trinity Street, as is their children's branch. Other more specialist branches are dotted around the city centre. **Cambridge University Press**, the oldest university press in the world, also has a shop opposite the Senate House. Antiquarian booksellers **Deighton Bell**, also in Trinity St, will search for out-of-print volumes on request. Other second-hand bookshops include the two branches of **G David**, one specializing solely in antiquarian books, which can be found in St Edward's Passage, as can the intriguingly-named Haunted Bookshop. If these fail you, try **The Bookshop** in Magdalene Street, and **The Green Street Bookshop**, which is (surprisingly) in Green Street, as are the rare books branch of **Galloway and Porter**, and **Brian Jordan** for music books. On the other hand, if you're after a currently published book, there are a selection of very good high street bookshops, including **Waterstone's** (Bridge Street) and **Dillons** (Sidney Street).

King's Parade is home to two shops which are linked particularly closely to the University. At one end stands the University outfitters, **Ede and Ravenscroft**, founded in 1689. Its windows display the ceremonial gowns it supplies to the dignitaries of the University. At the other end, opposite Great St Mary's Church, is gentlemen's outfitters **Ryder and Amies**, whose windows have been home to many University sports clubs' notice-boards for decades. **A E Clothier**, halfway between the two, also sells scarves, blazers, sports strips and umbrellas in college colours.

For ladies' clothes, **Troon**, on King's Parade, sells a selective range of designer-label garments. **Hero**, on Green Street, also sells designer clothing. as do the two branches of **Emporium**, in Green Street and Trinity Street. Other fashion shops can be found in Trinity Street , Rose Crescent and Bene't Street. Just at the end of Bene't Street, in Peas Hill, is **Raw**, which sells a wide selection of often wierd and wonderful 'Doctor Marten' boots. **Anohki**, just off Market Square, specialises in clothes a bit different to the usual high street fare with an array of colourful knits.

Every day, except Sunday, Cambridge's **Market** provides an alternative way to shop. Stalls selling everything from fresh fruit to old books and from secondhand clothes to fresh fish are open most days. On Saturdays, a **Craft Fair** takes place in All Saints' Passage (opposite Trinity College), and other art and craft events take place quite often in the Guildhall and Fisher Hall, both situated next to the market. Oriental food enthusiasts can buy authentic ingredients and genuine equipment at **the Oriental Shop** on Newnham Road (next to Sala Thong) and at their other branch off Napier Street.

For the antique and curiosity hunter, King's Street is particularly rich in interesting shops. Of particular note is **Primavera,** selling art from handmade cardes and jewellery to paintings and sculptures. Alternatively, if kilims and Afghan clothing are to your taste, **Nomads** in King's Parade is ideal: its wares are mainly from Central Asia and there are many fascinating items to browse over. If you are looking for serious art, **The Gallery on the Cam**, housed in an ingeniously converted river-boat near Jesus Lock (access from Chesterton Road) is a must. Similarly, **Sebastian Pearson**, in Free School Lane, the **CCA Gallery** in Trinity St reet, and the **Lawson Gallery** on King's Parade deal in fine art and rare prints.

Out of Town

T here is more to Cambridgeshire than just the City of Cambridge. The area round about has a rich cultural heritage, and if you have a few days to spend, you could do worse than escape the bustle of the town centre and range further afield. Here are just a few of the best sights and sites.

Near Cambridge

C losest of all the delightful villages clustered around Cambridge is **Grantchester**. (See walk three for more details.) Between Grantchester and the neighbouring village of **Trumpington** lies **Byron's Pool**, a pond where the poet often bathed while an undergraduate at Trinity College.

Three miles west of Cambridge along the A1303 lies the quiet village of **Madingley**. Near the village are the 16th-century **Madingley Hall**, where the fleeing Charles I stayed, and England's only **American Military Cemetery**. Open daily, the cemetery's hauntingly landscaped grounds provide the resting place for 3,811 American servicemen, who died while operating from British bases during World War II, and its Memorial Wall carries the names of 5,215 servicemen whose graves are unknown.

The Cemetery,
Madingley

Ancient earthworks can be found on Cambridge's **Gog Magog Hills** (two miles south of the city along the A1307). **Wandlebury Ring** is the remains of a first-century Iron-Age hill fort. The building in its centre is the stable block of a 18th-century mansion; it covers the grave of the horse Godolphin Arab, forebear of many English racehorses, who was buried there in 1753.

Just on the edge of the tiny village of **Lode,** five miles north-east of Cambridge along the B1102, stands **Anglesey Abbey**, Tel: (01223) 811200, a beautiful mansion built in the 1590s on the site of a 12th century Augustinian priory. Owners have included Sir George Downing, founder of Downing College in Cambridge, and Lord Fairhaven, whose art collections are displayed throughout the house, and who created the spectacular 100-acre Georgian-style grounds.

Further Afield

*J*ungle Book fans should be prepared for the 25-minute drive to the former home of Kipling's daughter, Wimpole Hall (nine miles to the south-west along the A603). Started in 1640, the house was completed in the 18th century, and the grounds were landscaped by Capability Brown in 1770. The landscaping involved the complete demolition of the original village of Wimpole, rehoused at New Wimpole, along the main road.

Nearer Cambridge at Duxford Airfield (8 miles south of Cambridge, off Junction 10 on the M11) is the **Imperial War Museum**. Lurking in the hangars are more than 100 aircraft, ranging from crude bi-planes to the prototype Concorde. For the intrepid, flights around the airfield are sometimes on offer, and there's always the consolation of the flight simulator for those who want to do the driving. The museum also has exhibitions featuring midget submarines and other fascinating details of military developments over the last hundred years.

For those who prefer leopards to weaponry, a visit to **Linton Zoo** is a must. Ten miles south-east of Cambridge along the A1307, the ten-acre family-run Zoo houses bears, owls, lynxes, the rare Indian eagle owl and the binturong (a long-haired Asian mammal), all in well-maintained grounds.

A little further afield (fifteen miles south along the A130) is the beautiful mediaeval town of **Saffron Walden**. Its name is taken from the Saffron crocus, grown here for its orange dye until late last century, which appears on the town's coat of arms. The town also benefited greatly from the wool trade, and its imposing church bears witness to its wealth and prosperity during mediaeval times. The town's many surviving 16th-century houses boast striking displays of 'pargeting' (ornamental plasterwork), especially in Church St. One mile west of Saffron Walden stands the magnificent 17th century Jacobean **Audley End House** (Tel: 0799 522399). Originally three times its present size, it was dubbed by James I as "too large for a king". The interiors have benefited from the talents of Sir John Vanbrugh and Robert Adam, while the gardens were landscaped by Capability Brown. Rides are often available on a miniature railway which runs round the grounds. Fifteen miles east of Cambridge along the A45 and A11 lies the county's horseracing Mecca, **Newmarket**. Races have been held at the

(right) The Chapel at Madingley Cemetery

town since the first gold cup race in 1635, and the full story can be had at the **National Horse-Racing Museum** in the High St. For the less horsey there is the seven-mile **Devil's Dyke**, a 6th-century earthwork built to defend the Saxon inhabitants from hostile tribes to the south.

Ely (16 miles north-east along the A10) is best known for its spectacular 12th and 14th century **Cathedral**. Its remarkable octagonal tower can be seen for miles across the Fens, and seeing it gives sense to the old name 'the Isle of Ely', which dates from when the Fens where covered by sea and the town was an island. The town was once home to Oliver Cromwell, and more can be discovered at the **Ely Museum**, just north of the Cathedral.

Huntingdon (16 miles north-west along the A604) was once the county town of the now abolished Huntingdonshire. It was also the birthplace of Oliver Cromwell, and the **Cromwell Museum** provides a record of his life. It is housed in a former grammar school, at which both Cromwell and the diarist Samuel Pepys were pupils. Not far to the west of Huntingdon stands **Hinchingbrooke House**, a 16th century mansion which was once home to a branch of the Cromwell family. Built on the site of a defunct Augustinian nunnery, it is now a school, but is often open to visitors, with senior pupils acting as guides.

The Guide

Restaurants

Something Special

LE JARDIN
The Garden House Hotel, Granta Place, Mill Lane. Tel: (01223) 259988
The recently refurbished Le Jardin is an elegant and spacious restaurant which boasts an extensive range of high quality cuisine, including imaginative vegetarian options and a children's menu. The food is beautifully presented, the staff are courteous and attentive and the atmosphere formal, though not stuffy. The chances are that if you can afford it you'll love it.

PANOS RESTAURANT
154-6 Hills Road Tel: (01223) 212958

The intriguing mix of French and Greek influence can be explained by the roots of the husband and wife who run Panos. As a result, the menu, which contains many steak and fish dishes, may be described as eclectic but all options are delicious. The restaurant is split between two rooms, each holding five tables, many set into alcoves, which makes for an intimate atmosphere.

THE PEKING
21 Burleigh Street. Tel: (01223) 354755

The Peking is a small family-owned Chinese restaurant with a strong emphasis on the quality and the quantity of their cuisine. Service is friendly but can be slow due to the care taken in cooking. The surroundings are basic and slightly shabby which leads to an informal but slightly uninspiring atmosphere.

Key to symbols:

£
Inexpensive

£ £
Moderate

£ £ £
Expensive

No smoking

⌷
Licensed

Particularly good disabled access

D
Particularly good children's facilities

V
Vegetarian options

Vegan options

Takeaway service

RESTAURANT 22
22 Chesterton Road Tel: (01223) 351880
Closed Sunday and Monday
Famous as being one of the best (if not *the* best) restaurants in Cambridge, it certainly deserves its reputation. Serving first class and imaginative English food in the smartly converted front room of its proprietors, it has an exclusive air making it perfect for whenever you want something particularly special.

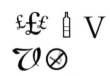

SALA THONG
35-37 Newnham Road Tel: (01223) 323178
Sala Thong is a small Thai restaurant which can be either relaxed or heaving depending on how busy it is. It offers both the usual fragrant, mouth-busting crowd pleasers as well as some subtler alternatives. It is definitely worth opting for a set menu (around £11 per head) or mixing and matching.

Student Favourites

THE BENGAL
4 Fitzroy Street. Tel: (01223) 351010
With friendly staff and a relaxed atmosphere, this is one of Cambridge's best Indians. Choose from a vast menu, if slightly more expensive than other Curry houses, the extra is well worth it for the dips and sauces that accompany many dishes. Also recommended by true experts - the Indian cricket team reputedly eat here on their tours to Cambridge.

THE BUN SHOP
1 King's Street Tel: (01223) 366866
This pub is a three in one - downstairs a wine bar on one side and a real ale pub on the other; upstairs a Spanish Tapas bar. The real ale bar serves traditional British pub food - from some of the biggest door step sandwiches ever to pub favourite; scampi and chips. All served at very reasonable prices. The Tapas bar serves fun food at good prices; a great place to go with a group.

(downstairs)

FOOTLIGHTS
Grafton Centre Tel: (01223) 323434
Despite being all the way out in the Grafton Centre which is regarded as another country by many students (although in reality a ten minute walk from the centre of town) it's still a popular place for parties due to the good Tex-Mex food and great cocktails. Informal and fun, Footlights is well worth a visit.

£ **D C**

V 🍾

Old Orleans
10 Miller's Yard Tel: (01223) 322777
A great place to relax and soak up the the vibrant atmosphere of the American Deep South, whether for their array of cocktails or the authentic food. Veggie 'v's' are very much in evidence on their jazzy menu which spans at least four pages. For meat-eaters, particularly recommended is the Blackened Red Snapper, presented at the table sizzling on an iron skillet.

£ / £ **C V** 🍾

Mongolian Barbeque
66 St Andrew's Street Tel: (01223) 361998
Choose your own ingredients for grilling on the barbeque, and go back for more as many times as you like; the Mongolian Barbeque offers great value for money and is great fun too. It's perfect for picky eaters, families, and for vegetarians too, as long as you're not fussy about having your vegetables cooked on the same griddle as the meat. There's also a bar, the Pleasure Dome, upstairs. Watch out for the ferocious cocktails!

£ / £ **C V** 🍾

Pizza Express
7a Jesus Lane. Tel: (01223) 324033
St Andrew's Street Tel: (01223) 361320
Neither branch takes bookings.
The all-time student favourite. Pizza Express are pizza restaurants, don't be fooled by the name, this is not fast food. The smarter location is certainly that on Jesus Lane, choose between the grand marble and mirrored hall or the more subdued bookcased drawing room and enjoy the un-intrusive piano playing. While St Andrew's Street may not be so classy, it serves the same high standard menu. The pizzas are Italian rather than American style and undoubtedly the best in Cambridge.

£ **D C**

V 🍾

Sweeney Todd's
Newnham Mill, Newnham Road Tel: (01223) 367507
With a massive menu ranging from burgers to pasta and pizza to steak, with a varied price range to match, it's a good place to bring family as it caters for a variety of tastes. Next to the river, the American country club style is relaxed. A great place for big groups, the emphasis is on variety perhaps at the expense of quality.

£ **D C V**

~~Tatties~~ *Sticky Fingers*
26-28 Regent Street Tel: (01223) 358478
Compared with many other fast food restaurants, Tatties is ahead on taste, originality and provides more for the health conscious. The range of toppings is huge, ranging from the standard cheese and coleslaw to garlic prawns and ratatouille. Theres also a good selection of tasty (if unispired) desserts.

Classic Choices

PASTA GALORE
5 Jordan's Yard Tel: (01223) 324351
Usually runs special offers such as £4.90 for a three-course meal at lunchtimes Monday to Saturday and on Sunday evenings. Shop sales of fresh pasta and sauces made on the premises. With its reasonable prices and cheerful atmosphere, decor and service, Pasta Galore can be described as functional yet friendly. The food is good, if simple, the menu offering pasta (surprise!), pizza, steak, vegetarian dishes and excellent home-made desserts. Also open throughout the day for coffee and tea.

RISTORANTE MOLISE
70 Newmarket Road Tel: (01223) 516716
Look out for £9.95 set menu Mon – Fri.
An intimate (but not quite cramped) little Italian with a wide selection of dishes and wines. The service is polite, the atmosphere relaxed. The menu has a handy diagrammatic guide to their pastas, but the highlight is Wednesday's and Friday's (restrained) live music.

THE RAINBOW VEGETARIAN BISTRO
9a King's Parade Tel: (01223) 321551
This small vegetarian restaurant offers an eclectic, though limited range of dishes in friendly, unpretentious surroundings. This informality, reflected by the open-to-view kitchen, doesn't stop the service from being efficient and polite. Considering the emphasis on fresh, organic food that could (and did!) satisfy even sceptical non-vegetarians, the prices are very reasonable.

(all areas)

(25% off)

(and gluten free)

GARFUNKELS
21/24 Bridge Street Tel: (01223) 311053
Conveniently located and spacious, the menu offers a comprehensive selection of the best in American food. Their mixed platters represent excellent value for money - large enough for even the healthiest of appetites. Garfunkel's has a great deal to offer the kids, including a special menu and a kids' goody bag complimentary with their meal.

HOBB'S PAVILION
Park Terrace Tel: (01223) 367480
Closed Sunday and Monday
The pavilion style restaurant overlooking Parker's Piece specialises in pancakes both savoury and wickedly sweet. Truly unique to Cambridge, it is obvious that a lot of effort is put into finding tasty new recipes. The food and service is up to the highest standard and makes for an unusual alternative, particularly for vegetarians bored with pasta. A must for anyone with a sweet tooth – the dessert menu is to die for.

(all areas)

PIERRE VICTOIRE
90-92 Regent Street. Tel: (01223) 570170
Feeling very almost authentically French, it does little to betray the fact that it is part of a chain. Serving an original menu the food is good and the prices are great if you take advantage of the lunch time specials. Also worth looking out for are the pre-theatre special deals; two courses for considerably less than a tenner.

£ £ 🍾 D V

Sandwiches, Lunches and Snacks

Peppercorns in Rose Crescent offers a galaxy of filled rolls, samosas and cakes, ideal for a quick lunch. **Fitzbillies**, on Trumpington Street, has an excellent upstairs café which offers interesting and delicious food at lunchtime and evenings, as well as its downstairs shop which sells sandwiches, baguettes, hot croissants and pasties, and the best selection of pâtisserie in Cambridge. **Trockel, Ullmann & Freunde**, on Pembroke Street, sell a variety of baguettes, organic drinks and sweet things, and a fascinating and esoteric range of cheeses.

Other good Cambridge cake-shops which also sell sandwiches include **Samuel Smiley's**, on Trumpington Street, and **Nadia's**, opposite St. John's College in St. John's Street. and on King's Parade. **Nichol's Sandwiches**, on Botolph Lane, sells the cheapest sandwiches in Cambridge.

Packaged sandwiches and salads are also available from **Marks and Spencer** (Market Square branch), who are famous for the quality of their food, **Pret a Manger** (opposite Christ's) and **Sainsbury's** (opposite Sidney Sussex College in Sidney Street).

Tea-Shops

Afternoon tea is a uniquely English tradition, now exported worldwide. 'High tea', at a table piled high with sandwiches, scones and cakes, has long been a favourite way to end an afternoon. Cambridge has a plethora of tea-shops, suitable for all tastes.

Auntie's Tea Shop, opposite Great St Mary's Church in St Mary's Passage, offers a full waitress service and a wide range of teas and cakes and can fill up during the summer. A quieter alternative is **The Cambridge Tearoom** on Wheeler Street, conveniently situated opposite the Tourist Information Office. **The Rainbow Bistro**, the excellent vegetarian and vegan restaurant in King's Parade, sells full cream teas for £5.95. **Fitzbillies** also serves tea and cakes, as do **Henry's** in Pembroke Street.

For those prepared to forego the convenience of waitress service, the choice widens. Directly across King's Parade from King's College is **The Copper Kettle**. This is one of the better self-service tea-shops, a popular student haunt, and an excellent place from which to watch the people passing by the windows. Other self-service tea-shops include **Belinda's** in Trinity Street and **Eaden Lilley's** 'Food Hall' in Green Street.

Best of all the tea places around Cambridge, however, must be **The Orchard Tea Garden** in Grantchester (see walk, p 48). Serving a wide range of teas and cakes, and also light lunches, seating is available not only inside but also outside in the extensive orchard on comfortable deck-chairs. The atmosphere seems to invite the visitor to spend the whole afternoon lounging around, and is reminiscent of the days when Virginia Woolf and Wittgenstein took tea in the same place. Regrettably, the Tea Garden is under threat from property developers, and may not be in Grantchester much longer – if it is still there when you read this, make the most of it while it lasts!

Cafés

Cambridge boasts a number of more cosmopolitan places for a coffee, croissant or a chat. Most 'studenty' are **Clowns** in King Street and Martin's Coffee House at the end of Trumpington Street. Clown's, open until midnight, is run by Italians, and serves an excellent espresso and cappucino, as well as quiches, salads and toasted sandwiches. It is usually crowded during termtime. Martin's is a popular refuge for students from the Architecture and History of Art faculties opposite. Other cafés include **Don Pasquale** on Market Square and **Café Carrington** on Market Street. **Trockell, Ulmann and Freunde**, on Pembroke Street, also serve coffees, teas, croissants and cakes.

Many pubs, such as **The Eagle** in Bene't Street and **The Mitre** in Bridge Street, also serve coffee.

Fast Food and Take-Aways

Cambridge has its fair share of the usual fast food outlets. These include **Burger King** (St. Andrew's Street), **Pizzaland** (Regent Street), and two **Pizza Huts**, also on St. Andrew's Street and Regent Street. **McDonald's** can be found in Rose Crescent, complete with mock ruins in the centre of the restaurant.

However, there are some fast-food outlets with a great deal more character. Most popular with students, especially late at night, is **The Gardenia Restaurant** in Rose Crescent (it is open until 3 a.m.).

Whilst the usual burgers and pizzas are available, it is predominantly a greek restaurant, serving kebabs and filled pitta breads. All are cooked with imagination and flair, and few students make it through their time at Cambridge without several trips to 'Gardies'.

Other places to grab fast food in the daytime are from the burger and hot dog stands on Sidney Street and at the corner of Emmanuel Street and Regent Street. The latter is often particularly good, serving food such as barbecued chicken satay rolls and steak sandwiches.

Pubs

Pubs are almost ten-a-penny in central Cambridge. Most of them are owned by the Greene King and Whitbread breweries, although there are a few independent 'free houses' which stock more varied and individual ranges of beers. The choice below is a biased and exclusive selection of our favourite pubs, based on the experience of living as students in Cambridge.

One of Cambridge's largest pubs, and one that every student knows, is **The Anchor** on Silver Street, opposite Queens' College. Inside, drinkers can enjoy a pint on any of the pub's three levels, the lowest of which is often loud and packed in the evenings. The pub has jazz nights upstairs on Tuesday nights, with a cover charge. Outside, there is a terrace right on the Cam, with space for punts to tie up nearby.

Just across the road is **The Mill**, well known for its wide range of well-kept 'real ales' which change weekly, and ferociously strong organic scrumpy. Take a look at the blackboard behind the bar to find out which beers are in. A wide range of fruit wines are also stocked. The Mill is particularly pleasant in the summer, when it is possible to take a drink out onto Sheep's Green, the green space opposite, close to the river. Many students choose this pub to celebrate the end of their exams. If you are drinking outside, remember to ask for a plastic glass. **The Granta**, on Newnham Road, next to the Mill Pond, is a large, modern, split-level pub with terraces overlooking the river.

At the other end of the Backs, near Jesus Green, stands **The Spade and Becket.** This has a modern feel. You can sit in the extensive covered bar, or, in the summer, go outside and watch the punts weaving their way down to the lock. A little further along the river is **The Fort St. George**, which until the seventeeth century stood on an island in the middle of the Cam. It is now firmly attached to the banks, on the edge of Midsummer Common. The food is good, and there are sometimes barbecues outside on the terrace in the summer. **The Boat House**, on Chesterton Road, has plenty of seating outside and in, and it is a good place to watch college

(right) You will never go thirsty in Cambridge

boat crews plying up and down the river in term time.

Away from the river, in the city centre, stands **The Eagle**. An enormous place, it belies its recent refurbishment, as the whole interior has been designed to reflect the long history of the pub. Cambridge was once even more full of inns and hostelries, as it was a major trading centre and inland port, and there was great demand for lodgings, stables, refreshment and entertainment for travellers passing through. The Eagle is one of the few places which retains its courtyard, where coaches would pull in to change horses and pick up passengers. The pub was also a favourite with air pilots in the Second World War, a fact which is reflected in the signatures covering the roof of the aptly-named Air Force Bar. Fighter and bomber pilots from the nearby airfields would go to The Eagle to relax, and signed their names, or that of their squadron, on the ceiling. Whilst the Eagle is sometimes packed, and is more expensive than some of its competitors, it is definitely worth a visit. It is open all day, and serves food.

The Mitre and **The Baron of Beef** stand next door to each other on Bridge Street. Both are regular haunts for students from neighbouring St John's College. The Mitre is mid-sized and quite modern, a popular place to be at lunchtime. The Baron of Beef has a very traditional atmosphere, with a good set of regulars. It boasts a bar which is said to be the longest in Cambrisge, a piano and bar billiards. Just across Magdelene Bridge and right opposite Magdalene College is **The Pickerel Inn**, which serves a good range of food at lunchtimes. This was once the alternative bar for Magdelene, and time was when every other drinker sported a college scarf or blazer. Things have changed, however, and today the pub is a pleasant retreat for town, gown and tourists.

The Maypole, near Jesus Green on Park Street, does an excellent line in cocktails. Mario, the landlord, has won national prizes for his cocktail-shaking. He also serves good food. The pub is well-known amongst students for being popular with the University acting community, as it is very close to the ADC Theatre. A little out of the centre, on King Street, is **The Bun Shop**, three pubs in one. Downstairs is a wine bar, which features occasional jazz nights, and a 'real ale bar', which serves a huge range of cheap and tasty food, including breakfast. Upstairs is a Spanish Tapas Bar. Further along King Street is **The Horse and Groom**, which serves the largest fried breakfast in Cambridge, and the cosy, traditional Champion of the Thames. King Street once had far more than its present handful of pubs, and the traditional name for a 'pub crawl' involving a pint in every one was 'The King Street Run.'

If you are prepared to go a little out of the centre of Cambridge, there are a handful of excellent pubs which merit the walk. **The Free Press** in Prospect Row, behind the Police Station on the far side of Parker's Piece, is a hidden treasure. Quiet, with superbly-kept real ales and log fires and candles in the winter, it also serves good food. Watch out for the rabbits in the backyard garden, and the smallest 'snug' in Cambridge. Please note that it is a smoke-free pub.

Both **The Clarendon Arms**, in Clarendon Street (again, near Parker's Piece), and the Panton Arms, in Panton Street (off Lensfield Road), serve large, economically-priced traditional English Sunday roasts. The Clarendon is a particular favourite with students from nearby Emmanuel College. Further afield, **The Live and Let Live**, on the corner of Mawson Road and Cross Street, has a cosy, local atmosphere without being hostile.

For the very adventurous, **The Phoenix** in Histon has the best Chinese food in Cambridge (book well in advance), and **The Wrestlers** on the Newmarket Road is the place to eat Thai. Both, however, get very crowded, and The Wrestlers' occassional live music is not necessarily to everybody's tastes.

Tourist information

Cambridge

CAMBRIDGE TOURIST INFORMATION CENTRE
Wheeler Street
Tel: (01223) 322640
Gives details of tours, including private group tours, as well as lots of useful information for the tourist. Please note that any group of ten or more persons wishing to visit the colleges must be accompanied by a blue badge Cambridge guide.

Other towns

ELY
Oliver Cromwell House, 29 St. Mary's Street
Tel: (01353) 662062

HUNTINGDON
% Library, Princes Street
Tel: (01480) 425831

SAFFRON WALDEN
1 Market Place, Market Square
Tel: (01799) 524282

PETERBOROUGH
45 Bridge Street
Tel: (01733) 317336

Hotels

Accomodation in Cambridge is usually difficult to find during the peak summer season, especially during 'May Week', (mid-June), around Graduation Day (late June/early July) and during the Cambridge festivals (late July). As a rule, it is wise to book well in advance.

This is by no means an exhaustive list of Cambridge's hotels, and inclusion does not imply our recommendation. More details of this and other types of accomodation, such as the YHA and YMCA, are available from the Tourist Information Office on Wheeler Street, which will also make reservations for you. Prices are intended only as a guide. Most hotels include the price of a full English breakfast in the room price.

(right) Wondering where to go?

ARUNDEL HOUSE HOTEL
53 Chesterton Road, CB4 3AN Tel: (01223) 367701
Single £39-£59, Double £55-£79

GARDEN HOUSE HOTEL
Granta Place, CB2 1RT Tel: (01223) 259988
Single £110, double £145

GONVILLE HOTEL (BEST WESTERN)
Gonville Place, CB1 1LY Tel: (01223) 366611
Single £77, Double £96

HAMILTON HOTEL
156 Chesterton Road, CB4 1DA Tel: (01223) 365664
Single £20-£30, double £40-£50

HOLIDAY INN
Downing Street, CB2 3DT Tel: (01223) 464466
Single £76, double £96

REGENT HOTEL
41 Regent Street, CB2 1AB Tel: (01223) 351470
Single £59.50, double £79.50

ROYAL CAMBRIDGE HOTEL
Trumpington Street, CB2 1PY Tel: (01223) 351631
Single £75, double £87.50

UNIVERSITY ARMS HOTEL
Regent Street, CB2 1AD Tel: (01223) 351241
Single £95, Double £115

Travel

Air

CAMBRIDGE AIRPORT
Newmarket Road. Tel: (01223) 61133
Air taxi service: contact Captain Richie at Cecil Aviation,
Tel: (01223) 294218
Tours and charter flights:
Magnet Air Services, Tel: (01223) 293621

STANSTED AIRPORT, *Stansted*
Offers a wide variety of national and international flights.
Tel: (01279) 662379 or (01279) 662520 for information.

The airport is approximately 30 minutes' drive from Cambridge, south along the M11

Railway

CAMBRIDGE RAILWAY STATION
For national rail enquiries Tel: (0345) 494950

Bus

CAMBRIDGE COACH STATION
Drummer Street
Intercity buses: National Express – Tel: (01223) 460711, Cambridge Coach Services – Tel: (01223) 236333, Local buses (Cambus) – Tel: (01223) 423554

Car Hire

Children's car seats can be booked from those marked (c)
Avis Rent-a-Car, 245 Mill Road Tel: (01223) 212551 (c)
Budget Rent-a-Car, 303-5 Newmarket Road Tel: (01223) 323838
CamKars Hire, 362 Milton Road Tel: (01223) 425706
Hertz Rent-a-Car, Barnwell Road Tel: (01223) 416634
Kenning Car Hire, 47, Coldham's Lane Tel: (01223) 61538 (c)
Eurodollar Car Hire, 264 Newmarket Road Tel: (01223) 65438 (c)

Car Parking

Warning: Parking in central Cambridge can be extremely difficult. Do not park illegally (on yellow lines or elsewhere), or there is a risk that your car will be removed without notice. The current fee for removal is over £100.

Parking restricted to 'pay and display' bays throughout central Cambridge 9am-5.30pm, Mon-Sat.

Car Parks

Short Stay: Lion Yard, Park Street, Grafton Centre
(Maid's Causeway/ East Road)
Long Stay: Gonville Place, Saxon Street, Gold Street
Coach Park: City Football Ground, Milton Road

Taxis

There are taxi ranks on St Andrew's Street and at the Railway Station.

Ivy-clad bike

Bicycle Hire

GEOFF'S BIKE HIRE
65 Devonshire Road, Cambridge
Tel: (01223) 365629

MIKES BIKES
28 Mill Road
Tel: (01223) 312591

H DRAKE
56-60 Hills Road, Cambridge
Tel: (01223) 634681

Horse and Carriage Tours

THE CAMBRIDGE HORSE AND CARRIAGE COMPANY
Spade and Becket Pub, Jesus Green
Tel: (01223) 360569

Travel Agents

American Express Travel Service, 25 Sidney Street (01223) 324432
Campus Travel, 5 Emmanuel Street (01223) 324283/360201
STA Travel, 38 Sidney Street (01223) 366966
Thomas Cook Travel, 18 Market Hill (01223) 366141/357356/367724

Alternative Cambridge

The following is a list of the shops which are recommended by The Little Green Book, the students' guide to being 'green' in Cambridge:

Oxfam, Bridge Street (clothes, stationery, cosmetics), Body Shop, Lion Yard (cosmetics), Culpeper, Lion Yard (cosmetics), National Trust Shop, King's Parade (gifts, stationery, cosmetics)

Cambridge boasts a dedicated 'green' shops; Arjuna Wholefoods, a co-operative, on Mill Road

Central recycling points are on Corn Exchange Street and by the car park on Park Street.

Help and advice

Emergency:
Dial 999 and ask for Ambulance, Fire or Police.

Hospital:
Addenbrooke's Hospital, Hills Road Tel: (01223) 245151

Chemists:

Boots, 28 Petty Cury and 65 Sidney Street Tel: (01223) 350213
Coulson Horace and Sons, 66 Bridge Street Tel: (01223) 353002
Lloyd's Chemist, 30 Trumpington Street Tel: (01223) 359449

Phone Line Services:

Citizen's Advice Bureau Tel (01223) 353875
Samaritans Tel (01223) 364455 (24 hour)
Rape Crisis Tel (01223) 358314 (24 hour)

Post Offices:

9-11 St Andrew's Street (Main Post Office, last collection
Mon - Fri 7.45pm) Tel: (01223) 323325
23-24 Trinity Street, 2a Trumpington Street

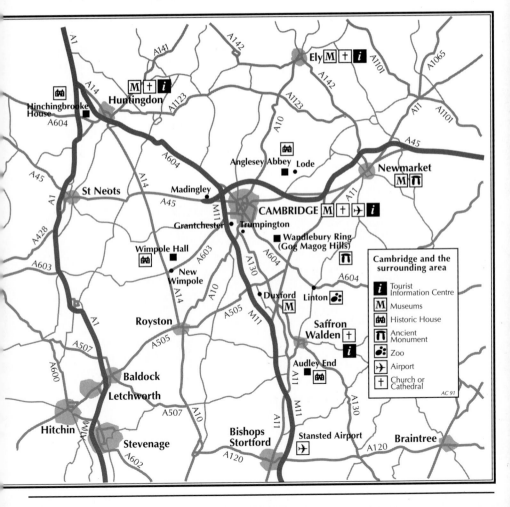

Also from Varsity:

*V*arsity is the student newspaper for the University of Cambridge. Produced every week of full term, it is written and designed completely by students and has won several national awards, including best student newspaper. *Varsity* is distributed free at all colleges' Porters' Lodges, but can be purchased from newsagents around the city.

*V*arsity Online is more than just the newspaper on the Internet – as well as all the news, articles and reviews from *Varsity* there are interactive competitions and exclusive multimedia features. It is available free of charge on the Internet:

http://www.varsity.cam.ac.uk

*T*he *May Anthologies of Oxford and Cambridge of Short Stories and of Poetry* were created to provide an opportunity for student writers at the beginning of their careers to see their work in print. Published each year, the books contain original work of undergraduates, post graduates and recent graduates, edited and designed by a student editorial committee, assisted by a guest editor, ususally an accomplished writer.

*F*rom our Cambridge Correspondent views the history of Cambridge from 1945 through the eyes of the student newspaper that recorded it. Tracing events from student protest in the 1960s to the admission of women to the previously all male colleges in the 1970s, this book provides a fascinating account of the issues that shaped the Cambridge of today.

*S*park is Cambridge's Arts magazine which features award–winning photography, poetry, short stories and drawings by Cambridge students. It is published three times each year.

VARSITY

Varsity Publications Ltd,
11-12 Trumpington Street,
Cambridge, CB2 1QA

Copies of the *Oxford and Cambridge May Anthologies, From Our Cambridge Correspondent* as well as subscriptions to *Varsity* and *Spark* are available directly by post.

For orders and enquiries, please send this form to:
The Business Manager,
Varsity,
11-12 Trumpington Street,
Cambridge,
CB2 1QA

I would like to order (please tick):

❑ May Anthology (Poetry)   £5.00

❑ May Anthology (Short Stories)   £5.00

❑ From Our Cambridge Correspondent   £6.00

❑ One year subscription to Spark (3 issues)   £5.00

❑ One year subscription to Varsity (22 issues)   £12.00

I enclose a cheque (payable to Varsity Publications Ltd) for: _____
(All prices include postage and packing within the UK)

Name:_____

Address:_____

_____

_____

Telephone:_____

Signed:_____